THE WAY OF LIFE SERIES

(A Series of the International Studies Conference)

THE SOUTH AFRICAN
WAY OF LIFE

The Union Buildings, Pretoria, Administrative Capital of the Union of
South Africa.

THE SOUTH AFRICAN
WAY OF LIFE

Values and Ideals of a Multi-racial Society

EDITED BY

G. H. CALPIN

under the auspices of the
South African Institute of International Affairs

COLUMBIA UNIVERSITY PRESS

NEW YORK, 1953

PUBLISHED IN GREAT BRITAIN, 1953, BY
WILLIAM HEINEMANN LTD.

This volume of the Way of Life Series has
been prepared under the auspices of the
International Studies Conference, on the
request and with the financial assistance of
U.N.E.S.C.O. The opinions expressed are
those of the authors and editors, who have
been given complete freedom in this respect.

PRINTED IN GREAT BRITAIN BY THE WHITEFRIARS PRESS LTD.
LONDON AND TONBRIDGE

Foreword

by A. L. Irvine

'For the past 150 years the history of South Africa has been a history of struggle and conflict. Conflict between black man and black man, between white man and black man, between white man and white man; struggle of white and black against a not over-generous nature—this is the background to its present problems.'

These words of Mr. Marquard's, which close the first chapter and begin the last, are borrowed without apology to stand at the opening of the book. They give the dominant theme. Indeed no better introduction could be made than by lifting a large part of the closing chapter bodily. For the strife motif is heard only too often. It is not that the writers write contentiously : they generally show great moderation, and where there is bitterness it is likely to come in the form of quotation. The South African Institute of International Affairs is by the law of its being debarred from taking sides; and, by the agreed condition of these studies, each writer advances his own point of view and speaks for others only as an individual, not as the accredited spokesman of a political party. It is in quotation that we hear from the Afrikaner Nationalist, Professor A. I. Malan (not the Prime Minister) of a fanatical will to survive—not by unity, but by dominating the British element—and that ' the matter of survival has become an irresistible life force, a veritable obsession ' (p. 137). We have yet to learn of fanaticism and obsession as wholesome things, and the will to survive looks here hardly less like a blind will to suicide. ' Why this fanaticism?' asks Professor Malan. Why indeed? It is far from the healing wisdom of Botha and Smuts. The latter, when Prime Minister, barred the civil service to members of the *Broederbond*.

Sport is declared to be the strongest and wholesomest bond between the two white races. One can only say, more power to their cricket and football !

The difficulties of the country deserve the most discreet and sympathetic understanding. The problems are too grave, and

v

the solution of none of them is in sight. Denunciation will not help to solve them, and it is a time for the vocal doctrinaire, in this country and in others, to hold his peace. Euphemeite, O Politai.

Men's lives in South Africa were simple and wholesome once, till ' catastrophe overtook them in the form of fabulous riches ' (p. 14): there followed the curse of urbanization, industrialization and the rest of the polysyllabic jargon. South Africa is now ' in the throes of its industrial revolution ' (p. 194), made far more deadly by differences of race and colour. Soil erosion, by Native ignorance, ' has now become a national problem ' (p. 167): a catastrophe from this cause ' is perhaps more imminent in the Union than in any other country ' (p. 168). And who shall ' exorcise the devil of fear '? (p. 197).

It is perhaps one of the functions of a Foreword to point to anything that seems to be of special interest. I would call attention to Mr. Currey's admirable sketch of Milner and the Kindergarten (p. 31); and when once the reader has met the name of Dr. van der Bijl, let him be on the alert to watch for it again. His contribution to the economic development of his country must be unequalled.

This study of a multi-racial society naturally asks for the co-operation of a good many hands, representing at least four nations: so we have here another ' symposium.' And the writers have formed their minds and drawn their sustenance from many sources: the biographical notices show, apart from the South African universities, past students of Oxford, Cambridge and London, of Harvard and Yale, and of Amsterdam. Mr. Marquard and Mr. Currey, authors of really distinguished chapters, were Rhodes scholars at Oxford. Dr. Goudriaan, before he left his own country, was General Manager of Dutch Railways, and spent two years as a hostage in German hands. Mr. Golding shows, at the age of forty-four, a notable record of work doing or done, and is the first member of his race to be appointed a Justice of the Peace. The Editor, Mr. Calpin, a former science master and house tutor at Durham School, England, and more recently Editor of *The Natal Witness,* is well-known in South Africa for his writings and broadcast talks presented in an outspoken manner.

A. L. IRVINE

Contents

Contents

List of Illustrations

CHAPTER I

Introductory

DAVID MARQUARD

THE people of the Union of South Africa form anything but a homogeneous group. There are roughly two and a half million people of European descent with a very high standard of education and of living; over eight million are members of the Bantu group, consisting of hundreds of tribes such as the Zulu, the Basuto, the Xosa and many others, of whom roughly half still live in tribal conditions and half as agricultural and industrial workers in European communities. Finally, another million are either Coloured or Indian. Although educational facilities for the non-white groups have developed tremendously during the last thirty years, these groups are still very far behind the Europeans in their general social, educational and political development.

In other respects, too, there is a lack of uniformity. About 60 per cent of the Europeans speak Afrikaans and the rest English. The climate of the country varies between desert, mediterranean, and tropical. About half the country has an insufficient rainfall; about half its total population is dependent on mining and industry and half on agriculture. In order to understand the complexity of its problems, it is necessary to know something of how they originated.

South Africa's geographical position and build have given to it a diversity of climatic conditions which has had an important effect on its history and its development. From the mouth of the Orange River on the west coast to Lourenço Marques on the east, there is a coastal belt which varies in width from 25 to 100 miles; thence the country rises in a series of terraces to the high veld or plateau which stretches almost into the tropics. The west coast lies in the desert area, and the coastal belt there is almost rainless. In the south-west the coastal belt falls just within the reach of the westerlies, and has a winter rainfall like that of California. But the whole of the rest of the country has a summer rainfall which is high in the coastal belt, varying from 25 inches annually round Port Elizabeth to over 40 inches in the vicinity of Durban. Roughly three-quarters of the country lies on the plateau over 3,500 feet above sea level where the summer rainfall of from 12 to 35 inches and the heavy frosts in winter give a prairie-like, treeless vegetation which is favourable to stock-breeding rather than to agriculture. The rain-bearing winds in nine-tenths of the country—the area of which Cape Town is the centre being the exception—blow from the Indian Ocean, and the rainfall consequently decreases as one goes westwards across the country. Northern Natal and the Northern Transvaal have a tropical vegetation, but almost the whole of the rest of the country is subject to at least ninety days of frost annually.

Until the great mineral discoveries of the late 19th century intervened, movements of population tended to seek areas of satisfactory rainfall. The great Bantu migrations which entered the country from the north-east after the 16th century tended to keep to the well-watered east and seldom penetrated further to the west than a north-south line drawn through the confluence of the Orange and the Vaal rivers, driving before them the physically and numerically weaker Hottentot and Bushmen tribes, who were gradually forced into the north-western and rainless portions of the country or into the mountains; the European settlement which arrived at Cape Town in the middle of the 17th century worked its way up the coastal belt towards roughly as far as where Port Elizabeth is to-day, eschewing the waterless interior and western coastal area.

The first European settlers were Calvinist Hollanders, reinforced by a small but important French Huguenot contingent and a steady trickle of German immigration, all of whom became farmers : in the Cape Town area where the winter rainfall was favourable they were wheat and wine farmers, but as they reached the summer rainfall areas they forgot their vineyards and measured their prosperity in terms of cattle. The general direction of their development was east and north-east, and in roughly 1750 they came into contact for the first time with the Bantu moving down the coast, the nomadic Hottentots and Bushmen having been squeezed out between the two stronger groups. There were great differences of colour, of religion, and of political organization between Boer (the Dutch name for farmer by which the white farmers came to be called) and Bantu, but there was one great similarity : both groups were dependent for their very existence on cattle farming and the extensive grazing it requires. By this time the Cape Colony had, as a result of the Napoleonic Wars, become British territory, and the first British immigration of 1820 was followed by a steady trickle which increased the white population requiring more land.

By 1836 the fight between white and black for land on the eastern frontier of the Cape Colony reached its climax, and the Boers, dissatisfied with the British government, which was strongly influenced by the philanthropists, and which refused to sanction Boer conquests of land from the Bantu, turned northwards in a mass migration which is known as the Great Trek; by treaties or wars or both they made themselves masters of the highveld (that portion of the plateau which is now known as the Orange Free State and the Transvaal) and of Natal.

This great grassland had for twenty years or more been the scene of destructive tribal wars, also for the possession of more grazing, the chief contestants being Bantu tribes like the Zulu under Chaka and Dingaan, and the Matabele under Moselekatse. The weaker tribes, like the Basuto, had gradually sought the safety of the mountains and had left a vacuum into which the Boer immigrants gladly poured and established their republican states of Natalia (1839), the Orange Free State (1854), and the South African Republic, later the Transvaal (1852). But the British Government, British missionaries and British settlers were not far behind, and in 1842 already Natal had been annexed by Britain, while a short-lived attempt to establish British domination over the highveld was made between 1846 and 1852, but was abandoned in the latter year during one of the few decades of the 19th century when Great Britain was not imperialistically minded.

This, then, was the position about the year 1870 : Britain in control of the coastal colonies from Cape Town to north of

Durban, and the Boers holding the country north of the mountains. And in between them and round them Bantu tribes; some of them, like the Matabele, now north of the Limpopo river, entirely independent of the white man; some of them, like the Zulu or the Bapedi, nominally independent but actually in the 'sphere of influence' of either Briton or Boer; some of them, like the Xosa near the eastern Cape boundary, by now completely under British rule. The whole population, except in the ports where there were embryonic industries, was pastoral. Boer and Briton, Zulu and Xosa, everyone lived off the land in a comparatively primitive subsistence economy. There was still a good deal of geographical racial differentiation. Most white farmers had, since the abolition of slavery in 1834, employed Bantu as farm and domestic servants, but there was as yet no breakdown on a large scale of that policy of racial segregation which had existed since white and black had first met. Missionary endeavour, from England, France, Germany and America, had barely touched the fringe of the Bantu population, which was still almost wholly illiterate and non-Christian. Nor had the Bantu made any attempt to acquire the habits, good and bad, or the norms of western civilization. The white man lived in a free, frontier-like independence, while the Bantu was still strictly under the control of his chief and his tribal organization.

Then came two discoveries which set the course of South African political, racial and economic history in an entirely different direction : the wealthiest diamond deposits in the world were discovered at Kimberley in 1870, and the great goldfields of the Witwatersrand in the Transvaal in 1886. The latter discovery especially came at a critical time, for the tremendous growth of international trade which followed on the industrial revolution throughout the world gave to gold, the prime means of settling payments between nations, a vitally important position. Once the permanence of these mineral deposits had been determined, men and capital began to flow into the country. In the political field the flag followed trade with a vengeance, for the diamond fields, which were in Free State territory, were annexed almost immediately by Britain, who subsequently made a compensating token payment of £90,000 to the tiny republic. Then, for fourteen years after the discovery of gold, Paul Kruger, president of the Transvaal, sought to run a modern industrial state with a governmental machine which had been designed to control a pastoral community. His vain struggle to retain his country's independence culminated in the Anglo-Boer war of 1899-1902, in which the Transvaal and its sister republic of the Free State were defeated and became British territory. This war, in which the name of Christiaan de Wet became world-famous, left deep scars on the vanquished and is now, half a century later, still a factor causing acute racial feeling between the two main white sections of the population.

Socially and economically, too, the discovery of gold fundamentally altered South Africa. The deep-level mines of the Rand could only be worked by European capital and management, which came in the main from England, by adequate coal supplies, which were fortunately close at hand, and by a large and cheap labour force. Attempts to introduce this labour force from overseas countries, including China, failed, and the Bantu of the country were called upon in large numbers to take the gold and the coal out of the bowels of the earth, to build the railways which were to link the new mining areas with the ports and with the agricultural districts, to build the roads and the power stations, the houses and playing fields for the new cities which sprang up—in short, to become the unskilled labour force of South Africa. And when the mining development was followed, in the first half of this century, by the development of a steel industry and of a number of secondary industries, it was again European capital and managerial ability plus Bantu labour which were called upon to co-operate. Thus the 19th century differentiation was changed by economic need to 20th century integration in the field of industry and mining. But not in the field of social and human relationships, where separate townships and first moral and later legal sanctions against integration in the fields of marriage, sport, religion and education were laid down by the Europeans of the country. The accompanying urbanization of millions of Europeans and Bantu, who had to abandon the well-controlled life of a pastoral or a tribal society and adapt themselves to the conditions of a great industrial community, has brought in its train problems which are common to all countries which have had the birth pangs of modern industrial-

ism; what is perhaps unique is that in South Africa these problems are intensified by the diverse elements which go to make up
the new urban population. In some sections of the country,
notably in mainly English-speaking Natal, the presence of a large
Indian population, originally introduced as indentured workers
to till the sugar plantations, complicates the problems still
further.

Eight years after the Anglo-Boer War, that is in 1910, the
four colonies federated to form the Union of South Africa, a
legislative union in which the powers of the provincial parliaments are negligible. In the country, as in the Union parliament,
Afrikaans-speaking citizens outnumber English-speaking citizens
in the ratio of roughly three to two. The growth of the Afrikaans
language, especially in this century, from a spoken dialect to a
modern language well equipped to cope with modern scientific
development, has been one of the factors which has encouraged
the growth of Afrikaner or Boer nationalism; both Afrikaans and
English are official languages of the country. Since 1910, too,
the Afrikaner element, previously predominantly agricultural,
has flocked in increasing numbers to the bigger cities and has
taken its place in industry and commerce, while every Prime
Minister and every leader of the opposition has, since Union,
borne an Afrikaans name. Since Union, South Africa has
shared in the development of the modern British Commonwealth
of Nations; in fact two of its Prime Ministers in General Hertzog
and General Smuts have played a leading part in that development.

For the past 150 years the history of South Africa has been a
history of struggle and conflict. Conflict between black man and
black man, between white man and black man, between white
man and white man; struggle of white and black against a not
over-generous nature—this is the background to its present
problems.

DAVID MARQUARD

Born Orange Free State, 1903, son of a Dutch Reformed Church
minister. Educated Grey College School, Bloemfontein; Grey
University College, Bloemfontein (B.Sc. 1922). Won a Rhodes

Scholarship to Oxford where he read Modern Greats at New College. Teacher at Grey College in Mathematics and History. One-time President of the National Union of South African Students, whom he represented at international student congresses in Europe in 1927 and 1928.

CHAPTER II

The Afrikaans-speaking Section

DR. S. J. DU TOIT

THE history of the Afrikaans-speaking section of the South African nation really begins on that memorable Saturday, April 6th, 1652, shortly after dusk, when two of the three ships that had brought the Dutch commander Jan van Riebeek and his hundred-odd followers to the Cape dropped anchor in Table Bay.

It had never been the intention to found a colony for Europeans here at this time. 'The founder of South Africa in spite of himself,' van Riebeek has been called by one of his biographers. The instructions of his masters, the Dutch East India Company, were simple and direct: he had to build a fort for protection and raise vegetables and barter meat for the revictualling of their fleets to and from the East. Little could they have surmised, that tiny band of men, as they stepped ashore under the shadow of Table Mountain, that they were actors in a drama unique in modern history. At a time when Europe, like dead coral, had ceased to grow new races and new languages, they were standing at the cradle of a new people with a new speech; an enigma; a sport of history and nature; an anachronism, if you like; or a miracle of God, as the Afrikaners, a deeply religious people, choose to see it—the only instance, since the days of Carthage and Greece, of a White community to settle, survive and retain its identity on the Continent of Africa.

The practice, a few years later, of gradually releasing a small number of soldiers and servants of the Company, the so-called Free Burghers, and granting them land to farm on, did not amount to a change of policy, a change-over to unlimited colonization. It was devised to meet a practical need. The supply of stock for slaughter, bartered from the aboriginal Hottentots, had proved precarious and uncertain. It was to

8

supplement the vegetables from the Company's gardens and to raise stock that they were given land. They were not meant to be the first settlers of a future colonial state. On the contrary, the effort to keep the expansion of the settlement within bounds was exerted, with more or less success, during the entire period of Dutch rule at the Cape, and continued later into the 19th century by the English. In the upshot it probably changed to a remarkable degree the course of events in South Africa.

Till 1707 the settlement, which had meanwhile spread beyond the Cape Peninsula, was not allowed to expand beyond the first range of mountains that hem in the Boland (Up-country). This stretch of country, with its grain fields, orchards and vineyards, is the most beautiful part of the Union, if not of all Africa, to-day; and it was here, amidst the grandeur of mountain, plain and valley, that the new nation with its new language first began to take form.

In many ways the Boland with Cape Town in those days must have been a miniature reproduction of all Western Europe and the East, a veritable babel of tongues and peoples in its small way. There were the men of Dutch speech, speaking their various dialects, at a time when even in Europe illiteracy was widespread. Then there were the Low and High German mercenaries of the Company who, on their release from service, settled among and married into the Dutch families, speaking dialects identical with or in various degrees approximating to those of their wives. Throughout this period, too, there was a fair sprinkling of individuals from other European countries, still recognizable from the names their descendants bear. The army of the Dutch East India Company was the *foreign legion* of those times.

This community was considerably augmented, and probably the confusion of tongues worse confounded, when towards the last decade of the 17th century the directors of the Dutch East India Company decided to send, from among the French Huguenots who had sought refuge in Holland, a number of families as farmers to the Cape. Some of the older members, we know, succeeded in mastering the Dutch idiom. At best it must have been difficult in surroundings where heterogeneous ingredients were simmering.

The Dutch which the aboriginal Hottentots and Bushmen spoke, or tried to speak, could not have improved intelligibility; there must have been many of them here, between the mountains and the sea, and their numbers were constantly swollen by clansmen moving in as seasonal workers from beyond, and a growing body of government and domestic slaves from the tropical coasts of Africa, from Madagascar and the East. Some probably could speak the Malay-Portuguese *lingua franca* of the Eastern seas. In course of time most of these elements coalesced into the Coloured population of to-day, close on a million Afrikaans-speaking individuals, but at that time their speech must have added to the general confusion.

It stands to reason that, amidst such surroundings, some kind of common idiom, some average between the extremes, a local *lingua franca* almost, had to take shape. It took the road that English followed under similar conditions during the centuries after the Norman Conquest, incorporating new words, playing havoc with inflexions, in general liberating itself from the tyranny of grammar, but remaining basically Dutch to a much larger extent than English remained Anglo-Saxon, or Middle English for that matter. ' In so far as Afrikaans is not the spontaneous development of Dutch,' says Dr. D. B. Bosman in his study on the origin of Afrikaans, ' it is a development of Dutch mainly under the influence of the Dutch of strangers.'

We do not know how far this development had advanced when, shortly after the close of the 17th century, the population began to spill over the brim of the mixing bowl which the Boland had been. Certain peculiarities of pronunciation, intonation and vocabulary, which distinguish the speech of the Bolander from that of his compatriot across the mountains, seem to show that the process could not have been completed.[1] The pattern, however, must already have been laid.

It has been said that 1707 is the year when the stock farmer made his real début on the stage of South African history. It was what one historian has called the beginning of the First Great Trek; for this was the year when, at long last, the colonists

---

[1] ' To-day Afrikaans can easily be distinguished from Dutch, but it is impossible to say from which particular point of time we have to do with Afrikaans as a separate language.'—Dr. D. B. Bosman, *Oor die Ontstaan van Afrikaans*.

were officially allowed to cross the mountains, through the Tulbagh Gap, and take up farms on the other side. They must have been very different by now from the Dutch-speaking officials in the Castle at the Cape. The generic term *boer* (farmer), originally used to distinguish the countryman from the townsman, was gradually acquiring an additional connotation and becoming an epithet of nationality. Spelt with a capital letter, it is still being used as a synonym for the probably more recent term *Afrikaner*.

The world was all before them. Nobody barred the way. The Hottentot tribes, never numerous, were all but exterminated by an epidemic of smallpox in 1713 and counted no longer. It was a slow infiltration which gradually dotted the country with scattered farmsteads, mostly eastwards, ever farther away from Table Mountain which anchored South Africa to civilization and the great world beyond. Distance and isolation accelerate change. This and their mode of life soon differentiated these pioneers from their compatriots back in the Boland. Their dwellings changed. The gabled Cape-Dutch houses became fewer and yielded place to tents and makeshift Hartebeest houses. On trek the tilted ox-wagon was really the residence of the Boer. It was a movable home when one farm was abandoned for another or when drought or danger drove the owner forth.

This trek occupied most of the 18th century. It was in the neighbourhood of 1779 that the stream of pioneers, meandering eastward, met another stream of immigrants, that of the Bantu, a people from Central Africa, who had been moving south while the Portuguese were discovering and the Dutch settling in South Africa. They met along the Great Fish River, Boers and forward bands of Bantu. The hundred years' war between black and white had begun.

In Europe the belief in the natural goodness of the 'noble savage' was still strong. Missionary zeal was at its zenith. The new masters, the English, who had finally annexed the Cape in 1814, were inclined to view the depredations of the tribes along the border, their incursions, cattle-lifting, plundering and murder as retaliations for ill-treatment by the Whites, the new English settlers and, especially, the Boers. This want of understanding and the state of insecurity which it occasioned in the eastern

districts is generally mentioned as the main reason of the Great
Trek to the north, which started in the years 1834, 1835 and
1836. There must have been other reasons. The rule of
strangers is never popular. Republicanism must have infected
the blood of these people. Their forbears had come from the
Dutch Republic. The American War of Independence and the
French Revolution were events which many could still remember.
Then there were geographical and economic reasons. Good
ranching land was becoming less plentiful; there was a great
drought in those years. At this very day Afrikaners in their tens
and thousands are leaving the Union where men of Afrikaans
speech have ruled for close on half a century, and immigrating
to territories where British and Belgians rule. There is more
room there. Also in 1836 there must have been a tangle of
many reasons, political, geographical, economic and human,
which made so many of those living outside the Boland decide to
cross the Orange River into the great void beyond.

There were, indeed, great empty spaces there. On some of
these no Bantu foot had ever trod. Others had been de-
populated some thirty years before in the wars of extermination
waged by the Zulu tyrants Chaka and Dingaan and the Matabele tyrant Moselekatse who lived beyond the Vaal River, and by
the *Völkerwanderung—Lifakane* the Basuto call it—which these
wars set in motion. It was only after the overthrow of these
tyrants, who had treacherously attacked the Boers and massacred
whole encampments, that the republics of Natal, Transvaal
and the Orange Free State (as it came ultimately to be called)
could be founded.

Natal was soon afterwards annexed by the English and became
in course of time predominantly English-speaking. The two
other republics remained Afrikaans. However, a happy-go-lucky
existence was out of the question. First the native problem
cropped up. Remnants of Bantu communities that had been
decimated during the *Lifakane* and in hiding, returned to their
former tribal lands or settled in new areas. Security under the
protection of the white man's rifle soon bred dissatisfaction : they
became resentful and recalcitrant. They were, after all, immigrants themselves, who had moved southward in the fairly recent
past, generation after generation, destroying or absorbing what

barred the way—Bushmen, Hottentots and other Bantu tribes—and must, like the Afrikaner, have felt the trekking urge in their bones. Their depredations, and the resulting coercive action and wars against them which occurred frequently during the early years of the republics, were but the counterpart of the series of Kaffir Wars on the borders of the old colony, where, even after the Voortrekkers had left, Boer and Briton had to face shoulder to shoulder, well into the last quarter of the century, wave upon wave of Bantu invaders that broke intermittently over the eastern districts of the country.

The Great Trek is regarded by the Afrikaner as the point on which the whole history of South Africa pivots. It has been commemorated recently by one of the most imposing monuments in the Southern Hemisphere. It conserved for occupation by Europeans the vast empty spaces of central South Africa, leaving to the Natives those areas which they were then occupying, more or less, and still occupy as reserves within the Union or as British crown colonies (Basutoland) or protectorates (Swaziland, Bechuanaland).

The new republics beyond the Orange River might have been described as pastoral states. But the Boers were no mere nomads moving from pasture to pasture. Travelling through the Orange Free State to-day one not infrequently comes across traces of habitations which their labours conjured out of the wilderness : a gnarled mulberry or a few century-old pear trees still white with blossoms, cowering beneath some broken-down weir or near a spring, long since dry and overgrown with mimosa-thorn trees, with wild asparagus, and with *wag-'n-bietjie,* where lush orchards and vineyards and patches of wheatland had once been, but where Nature has wrested from the feeble hand of man his brief dominion and resumed her ancient sway. *Naturam expellas furca, tamen usque recurret.*

By tradition they were really agriculturalists, these wanderers, like their forbears in Holland and their countrymen in the Boland, seeking a settled way of life wherever they went. Their culture, though rural, was of a high order, Christian and modelled on the Bible. They were Calvinists, and confirmation as members of the church demanded the ability to read and write. Illiteracy was therefore comparatively rare, even here along the uttermost rim of civilization. To their religion and high moral principles must undoubtedly be ascribed the fact, unique where aborigines far outnumber settlers, that they kept their blood pure; miscegenation meant and still means loss of class. To this almost caste-like raceconsciousness must, to a large extent, be ascribed the present-day colour bar conditions in the economic field outside the reserves.

The republics were well on their way to a modest prosperity when catastrophe overtook them in the form of fabulous riches. The discovery of gold and diamonds wrought havoc with their social and economic system. The gap between rich and poor became wider. It was like the Industrial Revolution in England. A purely rural community, the Boers found it difficult to adapt themselves quickly to industrial conditions. As the 20th century wore on, the Poor White Question, which was an almost purely Afrikaner phenomenon, became ever more acute. In 1920, according to the Report of the Carnegie Committee 1932, there must have been about 300,000 'very poor' people in a European population of 1,800,000. So it would probably have remained if the sudden spurt in industrialization during and after the second World War had not absorbed every available person.

The ethical impact of the new prosperity also was on the whole not favourable. It must be remembered that in the isolated settlement at the far-away southern extremity of Africa time had, in an almost literal sense, stood still, the further away from Table Mountain the longer. In their view of life the Afrikaners began to belong to a period earlier than that in which they were living. Nineteenth century materialism and scepticism which was searing the soul of Europe, and ultimately made its peoples run amuck in two world wars, did not really touch them. They were still a community traditionally stabilized in which values that were going by the board in Europe still retained their force. They were honest, hospitable and religious. They had a definite style of life. Into this world, like a bull into a china shop, broke the fierce spirit of the new age. An avalanche of strangers, alien in spirit and speech, adventurers often from every country of the western world, descended on them. They were soon outnumbered by them in the Transvaal. They brought the Anglo-Boer War and the loss of republican independence in their wake.

PLATE II

A. Groot Constantia, a Famous Cape Homestead.

B. Babilonstoren (1777), near the Town of Paarl.
In the background the granite rocks that glisten with a pearl lustre after rain,
and give the town its name.

[To face page 14.

PLATE III

A. The Voortrekker Monument, outside Pretoria.

B. Tulbagh, in the Rich Lands of the Western Cape.
Like all its neighbours, Tulbagh is dominated architecturally by the tall spire of
the Dutch Reformed Church.

It took the best part of half a century for the Afrikaner to adapt himself mentally and morally to the new view of life. Even now he has not wholly surrendered to it. In fact, many an Afrikaner movement now taking shape can only be explained as a reaction against forces which he looks upon as endangering his *ethos*. His church, even though split into three denominations during the 19th century, still exerts a unifying influence on his life and ways of thinking. It has been and still tends to be a force cementing all Afrikaners into one group.

The word TREK is writ large across the whole page of South African history. In the late 19th century the Cape ceased to be the point of departure; the Transvaal became the *point d'appui*. Treks set out for Bechuanaland, Mashonaland, Angola even. We have already mentioned the silent emigration at the present time to the Rhodesias, East Africa, the Congo. South Africa is agriculturally a poor country. Most of it is steppe and semi-desert. The rainfall, except in certain favoured spots, is small and precarious. Great droughts harass the land. Without gold and space South Africa, like Spain which it resembles, cannot support a large population. The Afrikaner chose space and trekked into the blue, ' because he knew a frightful fiend did close behind him tread,' the spectre of poor-whitism and poverty.

Of all his treks the most important was probably his mental trek into the land of the intellect. There, too, there was space. The first colonists who followed van Riebeek to the Cape were, like most of the common people in Europe at that time, in many cases unable to read and write. They signed their names with a cross. About a hundred years later the great majority of Afrikaans-speaking people could read and write the Dutch language in some way—we know the Voortrekkers could—however halting and ungrammatical their effort, and however brief their schooling might have been. Many had to gain their literacy within the brief space of a few precarious months, often from nondescript itinerant teachers : a Dutch sailor who had deserted, an old soldier, a stray Irishman even. Not infrequently these were shady characters. However, on trek and out in the wilderness one had to be thankful for small mercies.

In Cape Town and in the dorps the schools were better. After the English annexation of the Cape, Dutch soon ceased to be the official language and English medium schools were founded in the towns. The policy of the new rulers was to anglicize the population as fast as possible. The chances of achieving this ambition were not altogether unfavourable. Dutch, the written language, was no longer the vernacular of the Boers. Afrikaans, however, was looked down upon as a patois and was not written. To the townspeople of the first generation after the annexation, English became the language of polite conversation and familiar correspondence. It superseded and supplanted Afrikaans as the home language of not a few.

If we may be allowed to apply to this period the title of Julien Benda's book, although in a slightly different sense from that intended by the author, we could call it the time of *la trahison des clercs*. Those who had learned English at school began to fill the lower clerical posts in the civil service, in commerce, which was English, in private offices, in the railways later on. They also became teachers and, like the clerks, were proud of their English. They were the intelligentsia to the uneducated Afrikaans-speaking farming population and set the fashion. Also the republic recruited clerical and educational staff from these 'colonials.' Still the great mass of the people were not converted; most could, of course, not speak English, even if they would. Then Dutch, which they understood and attempted to use on appropriate occasions, was the vehicle of their religious and institutional life, and as such a formidable barrier. It is also a well-known fact that an intellectualized minority seldom succeeds in converting an integrated majority. In the end it is not the people that are converted but the ' clerks.'

This is what actually happened here. The Afrikaans movement drew its leaders from the educated. In actual fact these, supplemented by educated emigrants from Holland, a stream that had never ceased to flow, were the men who gave aim and purpose to the cause. Education became more general. Afrikaans-speaking persons entered the higher professions in greater numbers : the church, law, education, medicine. Lord Charles Somerset's attempt to anglicize the population had foundered on the reaction it called forth, and on British policy in South Africa during the 19th century, which called for ever greater interference in the affairs of the republics (the annexation of the diamond fields, the Jameson Raid, and the first annexation of the Transvaal), and ended in the last spurt of imperialism at the close of the century, when both republics were annexed after the Anglo-Boer War, which lasted three years and was accompanied by great material destruction.

In another sense the 19th century might be called an age of high ideals and lost causes. In Holland there were many dialects yet the whole nation could and did, when occasion demanded, speak the Standard Dutch (*Algemeen Beskaafd*) they had been taught at school. It was hoped that this Dutch might again become the spoken, as it was the written, language of the Afrikaner people, beginning with the educated and spreading gradually to all ranks. It did not seem impossible of achievement then. The 20th century has witnessed a dead language—Hebrew—becoming the spoken tongue of a whole nation. But Dutch was not a dead language. It was understood by Afrikaners and used as the vehicle for the spoken word on formal occasions. It stood too near and yet too far from Afrikaans. The literature it produced in South Africa was a failure from the artistic point of view. Dutch kept the Afrikaner tongue-tied.

That this was so became evident when, during the seventies, a number of intellectuals under the leadership of the Rev. Mr. S. J. du Toit formed, against great opposition from their own people, *Die Genootskap van Regte Afrikaners* (The Association of True Afrikaners), and started the publication of a journal in Afrikaans, *Die Patriot;* supplemented later on by *Ons Kleintjie.* This movement became known as the First Afrikaans Language Movement (*Die Eerste Afrikaanse Taalbeweging*). It did not yield works of high literary merit. The people still were too untutored. But it opened the floodgates of expression, and showed how a nation spoke if once it could do so in its own language.

The Anglo-Boer War and its aftermath put an end to the first *Afrikaanse Taalbeweging.* It had however sown its seeds. When *Ons Kleintjie* ceased publication in 1905 the second *Afrikaanse Taalbeweging* was already on its way. In less than ten years those still zealous for the Dutch language ideal were overborne in the struggle, and Afrikaans was introduced in the elementary school. The Secondary School, the University, Church and State followed. To-day Afrikaans everywhere enjoys equal rights with English. It already has an extensive and rich literature. Of some authors, like D. F. Malherbe and C. M. Van den Heever, novels have been translated into more than one language. Afrikaans poetry especially has shown great promise. Whilst the first poets (Celliers, Totius, Malherbe, Leipoldt) stand nearer to the 19th century English poetry and the generation of Dutch poets who started publication after 1880, a new generation of poets has now taken the field whose work falls into line with what has appeared in Europe and America between the two World Wars. An Afrikaans school of painting and sculpture also is coming into being—or shall we merely say that painting and sculpture have developed modern style and meaning? The eagerness with which the works of these artists are being bought indicates more than anything else the general level of culture attained by the public.

These are achievements peculiar to the Afrikaner on the intellectual side. But in other spheres which are not his alone, he has also made great strides during the half century now drawing to a close. The Afrikaans-speaking section has ceased to be a purely rural people, even though they still occupy as much or more of White South Africa outside the towns and cities as they did a hundred years ago. What has changed is that fully half of their number have become urbanized. South Africa has experienced the same mass-migration of her young men and women, from farmland to city, which caused disruption in the social pattern, both in Europe and America, since the time of the industrial revolution. The migrants who first moved into the cities to form a mobile population of the unskilled and the workless have been virtually superseded by a new generation. These are city-minded men and women, operatives, factory workers, skilled workmen, technicians, bank managers, mine and factory owners. Their children fill the universities, which are pouring out doctors, engineers, agricultural experts, economists. Big commercial concerns and companies, founded and run by Afrikaners, have sprung up and are springing up. The Afrikaner has become a Modern. His intellectual trek has probably been the greatest of all his great treks. He did it, not in the ox-waggon or bullock-cart, but in some time machine, catching up with Time and the Future which had left him behind. In one long bound he left the intellectual world of the 18th or early 19th century and, for better or for worse, has landed foursquare in the 20th.

S. J. DU TOIT

Dr. S. J. du Toit was born in the Orange Free State on June 18th, 1891, the son of a farmer-trader who had migrated to the Kimberley diamond fields from the Cape Province. The Du Toit family was poor, and it was not before he was twelve that Dr. du Toit was able to go to school. He obtained the B.A. degree in 1913 at the Grey University College in Bloemfontein, and shortly after that started teaching. In 1920 he went overseas and studied at the University of Amsterdam, where he obtained the degree of Doctor of Literature, his thesis being *Suid-Afrikaanse Volkspoesie, 'n Bydrae tot die Suid-Afrikaanse Volkskunde.* He was one of the pioneers in this field of study, and his book was hailed as something of a classic. In 1927 Dr. du Toit became an inspector of schools : and since 1945 he has been Chief Inspector of Schools in the Orange Free State. Dr. du Toit has published two volumes of poetry, *Uit Vreemde Boord* (1940) and *Tussen die Dae* (1947), and has written a large number of books for school use. He has contributed to newspapers and periodicals in South Africa and overseas in both English and Dutch, usually on educational or literary subjects. He is interested in psychology, vocational guidance and nursery schools, and is a member of Die Suid-Afrikaanse Akademie vir Letters en Kuns.

CHAPTER III

The English-speaking Section

RONALD CURREY

WHATEVER the Union has failed to do, and whatever hopes of 1910 remain unfulfilled, the disappearance from South Africa not only of the four British colonies but of anything that could be called 'the colonial spirit' is complete. That need neither surprise nor distress us. For indeed *there never were any colonies,* in the generally accepted sense of the word, in South Africa.

The original burgher settlers had come out, from Holland and the contiguous lands, in the days of the Company. Of their descendants, those who stayed on in what became 'the Colony' after 1806 and those who trekked beyond the Orange River and the Vaal and down over the Drakensberg, there is a full account in the previous chapter. Numerically smaller groups of British stock came out to the Cape through the next hundred years and more—in dribs and drabs. They came, or were sent, as officials and missionaries, as merchants and artisans, as soldiers and sailors; and many of them stayed on. Doctors and lawyers, engineers and schoolmasters, came out to ply their trades in a land whose own sons could only qualify for the learned professions if they had the energy and the means to go to Britain or Europe, to get there what they could not get at home. Only in the Eastern Province of the Cape in 1820, and in Natal nearly thirty years later, was there anything that could be called systematic colonization, and what there was was on a very small scale. At no time was there anything comparable to the wholesale emigration from Europe to the North American continent that was going on through the same period.

And of course it was only by annexation that the Trekker Republics became, even in name, 'British colonies.' Until gold was found on the Witwatersrand in 1886 the European population of the Republics was overwhelmingly Afrikaner. Overwhelmingly but not exclusively, for from the earliest days of the Republics the occasional Englishman or Scotsman was to be found amongst the Trekkers. He had got in ahead of them, here and there, as a missionary of the Gospel; he entered on his lawful occasions as a trader or prospector; he slipped quietly over the frontiers when his creditors weren't looking; he came in, more hurriedly and rather out of breath, as a deserter from some famous English or Scots or Irish regiment in garrison at Wynberg or Grahamstown. Most of them, especially these latter, became completely assimilated by inter-marriage with the people with whom they had thrown in their lot. To-day it is not unusual to find men with good Scottish names which they pronounce as one pronounces Afrikaans, and speaking English only as a second language and with difficulty.

With the opening of the gold mines of the Rand in 1886 there instantly poured into what is now Johannesburg that strange cross-section of humanity which the 19th century had already seen at Klondyke and Ballarat. But the Rand was not to prove a second Klondyke. Barberton and Umtali have followed that exciting, if short, road; but the Rand is different. If it cannot be said of it that, like Faith, Hope and Charity, it abides, at least it is indisputable that two generations after the first gold was discovered Johannesburg is still there, a vast city of American skyscrapers rising from the veld. Over its mining-camp memories time has shed a soft glow of romance, of which those who lived there at the time do not seem to have been specially conscious.

So to the Rand, in 1886 and the years that followed, men rushed. Adventurers of every kind, good men as well as bad, prospectors, American technicians, Cornish miners, youngsters from the Western Province of the Cape and the grandsons of those who had settled in the Eastern Province in 1820, other youngsters from Natal, traders, transport riders, dealers in liquor, men of enterprise and initiative who were prepared to take on a contract for anything, and—in the van of everything in South African history—an intrepid clergyman or two.

Behind, but only just behind, this motley army, and with

their scouts right up in front, came the big men, those whose concern was with prospectuses and flotations and options and syndicates. The first to come were of course the Kimberley diamond kings, Cecil Rhodes amongst them. They were almost on the spot, and they had the ready money that was required to develop the Rand. Others of their kind followed from Europe and America—Beit, Rudd, Robinson, Wernher, Joel, Barnato, Albu, Eckstein, with Abe Bailey and Jim Taylor and a few other young braves in attendance—the mere roll of names recalls the glory (or at any rate the glare) of bygone days. One looks instinctively for a Medici amongst them; and if Lombardy sent no knight to this latter-day crusade, neither Lombard Street nor Wall Street went unrepresented. For the gold of the Rand, following on the diamonds of Kimberley, had put South Africa on the world map, as people began to realize when the great Rothschilds themselves sent a representative to Johannesburg to report to them on what he found there. (His report was un-favourable : ' The broad reefs will soon peter out; the narrow ones won't repay development.')

Strange to recall, amongst those who came to the Johannes-burg of those days was that *beau sabreur* of Cape politics, John Xavier Merriman, half Galahad, half 18th-century Whig squire. For a brief period he was manager of the Langlaagte mine, but it does not seem to have taken the directors long to discover that their manager's great talents were being wasted in the company's service. Merriman did as much as any man, some would say more than any man, to establish on firm foundations in the land of his birth all that is best and noblest in the English liberal tradition; but he did not do this as manager of the old Lang-laagte mine.

So right into the very heart of the Trekker Republic there came the English, and not a few who weren't English. The whole process of history, it seemed, was being put into reverse : for here was Egypt crossing the Red Sea unopposed, and follow-ing Israel into the Promised Land itself. Just so, too, must the Ægean islanders have watched, bearing down on their shores, the sails of a little fleet of vessels from Athens or Corinth or Miletus. Aboard, instinct told them, were those who were coming to *their* island, peacefully or sword in hand as the occa-

PLATE IV

THE 'BIG HOLE,' KIMBERLEY.

he remains of the Kimberley mine discovered in 1871 and worked until 1914.
is estimated that diamonds worth £75,000,000 were taken from this mine,
which is 3,600 ft. deep.

[*To face page* 22.

PLATE V

A. THE WORLD'S LARGEST DIAMOND, THE CULLINAN, WAS FOUND NEAR PRETORI
IN 1905.

The large glass model shows the size of the uncut diamond. The smaller piece
represent the gems cut from the Cullinan which have been embodied in the Britis
Crown Jewels.

B. DRILLING THE ROCK FACE IN A WITWATERSRAND GOLD MINE.

sion required, not to trade or even on a foray, but to make their homes and to stay. Who were the newcomers, with their strange tongue and strange clothes and strange gods, and their terrible new arms?

> A flash of the foam, a flash of the foam,
> A wave on the oar-blade dwelling,
> And out there passed to the heart of the blue
> A chariot shell that the wild waves drew.
> *Is it for passion of gold they come,*
> *Or pride to make great their dwelling?*[1]

Just so did Paul Kruger and Niklaas Smit and Piet Joubert and the burghers of the South African Republic look askance at the strange tide of humanity that swept on to the Witwatersrand in the late eighties of the last century.

Nor for a good many years did the *Volk* feel the lure of Johannesburg. The European miners who took charge of the little groups of Natives, attracted to the strenuous and dangerous underground work by relatively high wages, were themselves recruited largely from the tin mines of Cornwall. For the first twenty years or so of its history ' Cornish Jack ' was a familiar figure on the Rand. The position to-day is very different. The overwhelming majority of the miners, and a high proportion of the mine officials, are Afrikaners. The change took place chiefly during the first World War. In 1913 there were strikes and riots on the Rand; martial law was proclaimed, the troops were called out, and there was firing in the streets. This happened again in the following year. Of the strike leaders, who were deported without trial, not one was an Afrikaner; of the rank and file the great majority were ' English-speaking.' Eight years later, when similar trouble had to be faced, there were Afrikaners amongst the men's leaders, and the rank and file were predominantly Afrikaner. For, by 1922, the Great Trek-in-reverse from the countryside to the cities was already well under way.

It was soon to become something like a torrent. It was to move not to Johannesburg only, nor merely to Afrikaner Pretoria or Bloemfontein, but to anglicized Cape Town, to the cities and towns built by the descendants of the 1820 settlers in the

---

[1] Euripides, *Iphigenia in Tauris*, 407 ff., transl. Murray.

Eastern Province, to English Maritzburg and to ultra-English Durban. Only a generation ago rural South Africa, except in the Eastern Cape and Natal, was almost entirely Afrikaner; but the towns, except for Pretoria and Bloemfontein, the Transvaal and Free State dorps and the lovely old country towns of the Western Province, were in the main English. To-day the proportion of Afrikaners in the town population of the Union is everywhere on the increase. In every town new Dutch Reformed Churches are rising; more and more one hears Afrikaans spoken in the streets; everywhere one sees more of it in advertisements and shop notices.

There has been more than one cause for this. As the towns have grown and the demand for town workers has increased, it is from the country, the *platteland,* that these demands have had to be met, from that platteland which is to the Afrikaner his spiritual as well as his material home, and which has for him all the religious and patriotic significance that the desert has for the Jew and the Arab. For never since the British settlers came to the Eastern Cape in 1820, and to Natal thirty years later, had there been anything but a drib and drab immigration policy to South Africa, until the short-lived enterprise after the second World War, which ended with the change of government in 1948. The enforcing since 1910 of bilingual requirements in the Public Service has meant that, forty years later, if one goes into a post office or police station or goods yard or magistrate's office and listens to the clerks and constable, porters and officials, talking amongst themselves, it is only Afrikaans one ever hears spoken. The present position, too, is to some extent the result of the activities of those political, semi-political and 'cultural' groups which have brought pressure to bear on successive governments, willing and unwilling, to give to Afrikaners their language and Church and way of life generally, all that these pressure groups feel to be their full national heritage.

Whether this policy has not been almost too successful, from its own promoters' point of view, is an interesting question; but no attempt to answer it need be made in this chapter. Here we have only to note the change that has occurred, whether with approval or regret does not matter. A generation ago, throughout the towns of the Union, the ' working classes ' (if one may still use that expression, with its quaint Victorian flavour) were mainly of British descent. To-day that is emphatically not so.

So, as things stand to-day, the former clear-cut, town and country, division of English-speaking South Africans and Afrikaners has to a large extent broken down already, and the breaking down process is still going on. It is still true that the former are in the main concentrated in the coastal towns, along the Rand, in the Eastern Cape and in Natal; but these areas have ceased to be their preserves. For the Great-Trek-in-reverse has now been well under way for two or three decades. To-day, to use the kind of political jargon which should only be used with caution when applied to South Africa, the 'urban proletariat,' so far as it is European, is largely Afrikaner, even in Durban.

We have to remember, too, that there is already a section of the European population of South Africa which cannot be neatly classified in either group, quite apart from those, such as the Jews, who definitely belong to neither. The number of these people is not easy to estimate, but it is certainly increasing. They are not merely bi-lingual, i.e., Afrikaans-speaking people who can speak and write English or vice versa. They are the people who are equally at home in either language, who use either indifferently as the occasion demands, and amongst themselves will switch from the one to the other without realizing that they are doing so. Of greater significance than this is the fact that such people have developed a way of life which cannot be labelled either Afrikaner or British yet is compounded of both.

It is mainly intermarriage which is producing such people, and will go on doing so. With a good deal of reason they may claim that it is they who are the real South Africans. Yet intermarriage does not always produce this type. Differences of circumstance and character may lead to the complete assimilation of one partner into the 'culture-group' of the other, to use for the moment the kind of language that so far has been carefully avoided in this chapter. In such a case the children are clearly and definitely either Afrikaners or English-speaking South Africans. Nor is intermarriage the only factor which is producing this new type. Many other circumstances are fostering its growth. Commerce, for long the monopoly of the British section and the

South African Jewish community, is becoming more and more a bilingual activity. The professions, especially Law and Medicine, have long been so. Sport is perhaps the most potent of all the influences that are bringing Afrikaner and Britisher together in the Union.

However, it remains true, and will be true for many years to come, that the bulk of South Africa's white population can still be classified as either Afrikaans or English-speaking. Exactly what proportion of the 2,643,187 Europeans enumerated in the 1951 Census belong to each section it is not easy to say. The complete Census figures will show how many unilingual people, of either kind, there are, and how many have described themselves as bilingual. But it would be unwise to make these figures the basis for determining how many of South Africa's white population are English-speaking, and how many Afrikaans-speaking, in their own homes. The term 'bilingual' is very differently interpreted by different people. A sounder basis is that provided by the figures of the different religious groups into which the population is divided. We are on safe ground in presuming that all the members of the three sections of the Dutch Reformed Church are Afrikaners, and that almost all the European members of the other Christian Churches are English-speaking. On this basis of calculation we may conclude with reasonable accuracy that for every hundred Afrikaners in the Union there are seventy-five whose home language is English.

But behind these figures there lies a significant fact of which we have to take account. A study of the age-groups of the two sections shows very clearly that the preponderance of Afrikaners over Britishers increases steadily as the age of the group drops. It is thus inevitable that the proportion of Britishers in the Union will steadily decrease, for some years to come at any rate, unless their numbers are increased by immigration. For, as things stand at present, in the average Afrikaner family in the Union there are a larger number of children than in the average English-speaking family.

The social and political implications of this need not be stressed.

It is possible that this may be due to other differences than those of race, and these may change with time. In South Africa, as in other lands, the European birth-rate tends to be lower in the 'higher income groups,' and vice versa. There is a good deal, in fact, to suggest that an undoubted difference in social habits is to be explained rather by economic than racial differences; and these differences are unlikely to be permanent.

It is, then, to be expected that ' English South Africans' will be absorbed or assimilated in a generation or two, and so disappear, and the white population of the Union thus become a homogeneous group. Will the tongue that Shakespeare spoke be spoken and read in South Africa only as people in other lands speak and read French for 'cultural' reasons, or make themselves proficient in Spanish to meet the requirements of commercial intercourse with South America? We may reply with confidence that this is not a prospect to be included amongst South Africa's reasonable hopes or fears. Mere numbers are against it. So are the ties of family connections, of commerce, and of intellectual and artistic interests which still bind Britain and South Africa. If America were not an English-speaking land the prospect in South Africa *might* be different; but into that hypothetical question there is no need to enter. The Englishman arriving in South Africa is certainly regarded by us as 'different.' Equally certainly he is not regarded as a ' foreigner.' Nor is the Canadian, nor the Australian, nor the New Zealander.

For lying beneath, and transcending the ties of blood, and the no less strong ties of commerce and of social and intellectual intercourse which bind South Africa, and not merely many South Africans, to Britain, there is something else. It is both a tradition and a heritage. It is seldom self-conscious; and those who are most aware of it and cherish it most dearly are least given to talking about it. It defies definition, and to describe it is not easy.

First, most obvious, and perhaps most important of all, there is the British political heritage. For what unites the nations of the British Commonwealth in a unity of approach and outlook, more closely indeed than the 'facts' of blood or history or common interests, is a fact of a different kind altogether. It is a political fact—the fact that we are all of us governed by an Executive itself drawn from, and responsible to, a Legislature we have ourselves elected. ('We' in this connection means white South Africans.) On the anvil of history the statesmen and the people of Britain have hammered out 'the British Constitution,' not without dust and heat, or blood either. The result is the parliamentary democracy we know—King, Parliament, Ministers, the Law Courts and the People. That Constitution in its essential form, and in due course with all its essential powers, law confirming at each stage what custom had first established,[1] is now in the fullest sense of the word *ours*. That this is so has had a profound effect on life as it is lived in the Union of South Africa. It has a profound effect to-day.

British parliamentary democracy was established in South Africa originally in the old pre-Union colonies. The Cape in particular had a long training in the habits and discipline which this system requires if it is to work effectively. The Colonial Parliaments were far from being sovereign legislatures; but they had the form, and soon acquired the spirit, of parliamentary democracy of the British pattern. As a people we have grown used to the idea of government by ministers responsible to Parliament. We know from practical experience the value of 'the Crown' in a scheme of things in which the arbitrary exercise of prerogative has been replaced by the influence with which the prestige of the office, and her own character and personality, endow the Queen, and which is transmitted to her representatives, the Governors-General. We know that the Opposition is an integral part of the political machine, and we allow no restrictions on its right to criticize. We do not allow the Executive to interfere with the Courts; but neither do we allow the Courts to declare any Act of Parliament invalid.[2] When a South African Cabinet Minister meets the Chancellor of the Exchequer or the Lord Privy Seal or the Lord President of the Council, they find that they talk a common language. So, too, do the members of

[1] The most important of the stages that have marked the growth of full national sovereignty in the Union have been the passing, by the U.K. Parliament, of the S.A. Act (1909) and the Statute of Westminster (1931), and, by the Union Parliament, of the Status of the Union Act (1934).

[2] This was written before 1952, when the Appellate Division of the Supreme Court declared invalid two Acts affecting the "entrenched clauses" of the Constitution which had not been passed by a two-thirds majority of both Houses of Parliament sitting together.

the House of Commons and the members of the House of Assembly. The two machines of government and law-making work just the same way.

This has deeply influenced politics and much else in South Africa. It has supplied the mould in which our public life is cast and it has trained us in habits of thought and action which are now part of our national character. To abolish it and replace it by some synthetic constitution worked out in the study by politicians and professors, as some would have us do, would be to do violent damage to that character. For political habits are plants of slow growth, and if one hopes to gather flowers and fruit of them it is foolish to tamper with the soil in which the roots are growing.

In this, America has a lesson for South Africa. The great Republic of the West is itself the child of Revolution. But it is significant, as Bryce has pointed out, that all the provisions of the American Constitution which have best stood the test of time and experience are just those to which Americans had grown used in the colonies out of which the United States grew. It is even more significant that most of the innovations introduced into the Constitution—the method of electing the President, for instance—broke down very soon and were either removed by amendment of the Constitution or else have become dead letters. It has been much the same in South Africa. In only two important respects did the Constitution set up by the South Africa Act differ from the old Colonial Constitutions. The Senate was deliberately modelled, in certain essential respects, on that of the United States; the provincial system on that of the cantonal system of local government in Switzerland. The stoutest champion of the South African Senate and Provincial Councils would hardly claim that either was amongst the most satisfactory or effective features of the Constitution. The reason is not far to seek. Each represents some strange, unfamiliar idea in which the ordinary citizen from the very start of Union has just refused to get interested, and which, forty years later, only the initiated understand. For our political system is that of the British Commonwealth, and a wise and deeply rooted instinct makes us resist and reject anything like fundamental departures from it.

Yet, very strangely in view of what has just been written, it is the Afrikaner who proved the more adept and zealous in the practical business of politics in South Africa. It is not entirely true that the English-speaking South African is so wrapped up in his trade and profession, his games and his clubs and his social life generally, that he just won't be bothered to interest himself in politics; but there is some truth in the assertion. Certainly in this matter he has a very great deal to learn from his Afrikaner fellow-citizen. At election times neither flood, mountain nor desert will hold up the Afrikaner on his way to the polling booth; but candidates know to their cost how hard it is to get a good many English-speaking South Africans there. We seem to glory in refusing to take any interest at all in the choice of the men who are to govern us, impose the taxes we have to pay, and be endowed with power to touch our lives at every turn during the next five years. Not the least hopeful of the signs of the times is the growing interest which the younger generation of English South Africans, many of them ex-service men, are taking in politics.

What is true of political life in South Africa is true also of the public administration and of the administration of justice amongst us. Our Government offices to-day are manned and directed predominantly by Afrikaners. So is the whole state railway service, with its virtual monopoly of public transport in the Union. So is the Union Defence Force, except—for the present—the infant South African Naval Force. But throughout all these services, the organization, method and system is that established in times past, either under British direction or on the British model. They were established through a century of 'Crown Colony,' 'Representative' and 'Responsible' Government, in their successive stages, at the Cape, and over half that period in Natal. Those were the days when it was complacently taken for granted that the methods of Whitehall must be the right methods everywhere, and that all one had to do was to copy them. (But admiration for Whitehall did not extend to Downing Street. On questions of frontiers and native policy, the Cape felt, one could almost take it for granted that Downing Street was probably wrong.)

So the small but competent machine of government was built up at the Cape through a hundred years of peace, for the

frontier 'wars' seldom upset the leisurely and dignified routine
in which the Cape Civil Servants lived their placid, useful lives
and administered the colony. To a small but significant degree
the service was recruited from England. The leading officials
long formed something of a social class in colonial society; and
the Civil Service Club in Cape Town is the doyen of such institutions in South Africa, though relatively few of its members to-day
are Civil Servants. As a Service it was rather more than reasonably efficient. More important even than efficiency, the integrity
of its officials established a tradition to which South Africa owes
much. It was essentially a British tradition.

North of the Orange River and beyond the Vaal administration necessarily took a different form. The Trekker Republics
established their own rather easy-going but effective system of
administration. In the Free State, particularly, this seems to
have been admirably adapted to the needs of a peace-loving,
pastoral people. The Transvaal from the start had a stormier
passage, and the sudden expansion of the whole machine of
government, made necessary by the discovery of gold in 1886,
and in the increase of wealth and the coming of the Uitlanders
which this brought, presented a problem of an entirely new kind.
This was met in part by President Kruger's importation of experts of various kinds from Holland. Some of these played a big
part in the stormy days that lay twelve short years ahead. But
three years of war and destruction, annexation and military
government, inevitably produced something only one degree removed from administrative chaos when peace was signed on
May 1st, 1902.

Riding the whirlwind and directing the storm in South Africa
at that moment of crisis there stood the genius of Alfred Milner.
It is not the fashion to-day to think of him as men think of
George Grey and Merriman and Rhodes, of Retief and Maritz
and Uys and Pretorius, of Kruger and Smit and Steyn and
Joubert, of Escombe and Robinson, of Botha and Smuts, and of
the others who have loved and built South Africa. Candidates
for Parliament do not seek to win votes by invoking Milner's
name and memory from their platforms; though indeed many of
them will refer to him with gusto as South Africa's evil genius in
those old, unhappy, far-off days. Yet to do so is to make a mis-

take. Immensely able, icily reserved, courteous, very much the intellectual, lacking in the broader sympathies, yet with something like a genius for friendship and for arousing the devotion and loyalty of those who served him, ruthlessly but selflessly efficient, Milner has cut his name deep into South Africa. Much of his work has perished; and he himself lived to see the triumph of his former foes, in South Africa and in England too. But much of it abides; and South Africa will only part with it to her loss and at her peril.

For into the chaos into which administration had inevitably fallen in the Transvaal and the new ' Orange River Colony ' Milner infused that order, efficiency, zeal and integrity which were part of his own nature, and amidst which he had worked as a Civil Servant himself, in Whitehall and in Egypt. As his lieutenants he brought out to South Africa that brilliant group of young men whom Merriman's impish genius dubbed ' the kindergarten.' At their head came Patrick Duncan, who was to die in office as Governor-General of the Union. With him came Lionel Curtis, John Buchan, Philip Kerr (later, as Lord Lothian, Britain's wartime Ambassador in Washington), John Brand, Richard Feetham and others. Devoted to their leader and working as a team, out of chaos they established order and in a short time prosperity followed. The gold that lay in the reefs of the Rand is only part of the explanation. Of itself gold does not bring order, or even general prosperity. Behind the gold industry there lay efficient, just and devoted public administration. In a few years Milner and his kindergarten built up a great tradition of public service in the newly-annexed colonies. To it they gave the labour of their lives; for they had learned that without sound public administration no land, however wealthy, can ever know anything but confusion and unhappiness. It was essentially the British tradition in such things, the same which others had been building up, more slowly and in greater peace, at the Cape. Half a century later sees it changed, developed, at many points deeply overlaid, directed by men to most of whom perhaps Milner's name is only an evil memory. But the foundations stand, and South Africa has good cause to be grateful that they do.

So, too, in the sphere of Law and Justice. By a strange chain of historical events the Roman Dutch Law of Holland has become the Common Law of South Africa, though it has ceased to be the Common Law of Holland itself, where it has been displaced by a legal system based on that of the Code Napoleon. The British found Roman Dutch Law established at the Cape, and at the temporary Occupation in 1795, and again at the permanent Occupation in 1806, they wisely decided to leave well alone. It was later adopted in Natal; it spread to Southern Rhodesia; and it is the Common Law of South-West Africa. With that history the Union's legal system might well seem to be the most un-English thing in South Africa, and indeed to have perpetuated an un-English, if not an anti-English, tradition strong enough to withstand even the deliberate anglicizing policy of Lord Charles Somerset.

Yet even against this background English legal thought and practice have deeply influenced the administration of justice amongst us. In the early days of the Cape Colony, and well into the last century, it was a usual practice for judges to be imported from Britain. Many young South Africans, on the other hand, enrolled as members of one of the English Inns of Court, or passed through an English university, in order to qualify as barristers in South Africa. Amongst these were the men, Lord de Villiers at their head, whose creative labours established not only a body of Case Law, but the practice, spirit and traditions of our courts, and imbued them all, deeply, with the spirit of English justice. This has permeated the interpretation our courts give to our Roman Dutch Common Law. It forms no small part of that English tradition in South Africa which is no less real, true and effective because we are seldom conscious of it and merely take it for granted.

In the deeper things of the spirit, too, South Africa has drawn heavily on the English tradition; and in this field English South Africans have made, and are making, their contribution to the country's national life. There is of course no Established Church in the Union, and indeed the picture is one of a bewildering and distressing variety of churches and sects, Christian and non-Christian, amongst European, Coloured and Native people alike. Nor amongst English-speaking Christians in the Union is there, alas, that homogeneity of doctrine, government, character and spirit which marks the three 'Dutch Reformed' Churches of South Africa, whose work is discussed elsewhere in this book. That work, over 300 years, has been a noble service of the God to Whose glory the Dutch Reformed Churches are built.

English Christianity, and English Christians too, have played their part in South Africa, and are playing it to-day. Anglican, Roman Catholic, the Free Churches ('nonconformist' has no meaning in the Union) have all been represented from the earliest days of the Occupation. In every church the work falls into the same two divisions. There is the pastoral work amongst the white and coloured congregations; and there is the work in the mission field, part pastoral, part evangelistic. It is in this field perhaps that the greatest work has been done by English Christians in South Africa. It is certainly the hardest work; and in it all the churches have played their part. Little known, overworked, underpaid, misunderstood, sometimes mistaken, often abused, their work crippled for lack of essential resources, the missionaries, catechists, teachers and doctors labour, year in and year out, in mission stations from the Cape to the Limpopo. Yet any fair-minded student of South African affairs knows that—in the long run—it is on them more than on the politicians that South Africa's future depends.

In this work English churchmen of all religious obediences have laboured mightily. First in the mission field, on any scale, amongst English Christians, came the Free Churches; and their missionary labours are continued to God's glory to-day. In the early days following 1806 the shackles of the Establishment seem to have cramped the infant limbs of 'the Church of England in these parts'; but with the coming of Robert Gray as first Bishop of Cape Town in 1847 the situation was transformed.

The Roman Catholic Church, august, venerable, unswerving, has its mighty network of churches, mission convents and schools throughout the Union. Against Roman Catholicism the ultra-Protestant prejudices of certain sections of the Dutch Reformed Church seem to die hard.

But when it comes to the written word we have to admit at once that the harvest of writers of English in South Africa is not to be compared, in quantity at any rate, with that of their Afrikaans fellow-craftsmen. In quality their work is often high, in more than one part of the field; and the field itself is widening fast. Certainly our writers of English have no cause to feel ashamed—and neither they nor their critics are able to forget that their work has to be judged, as has all English writing, against the background of the whole of English literature. That is a reflection which powerfully inhibits any tendency to boast of what is being done.

In his *Study of History* Professor Arnold Toynbee has much to say about minorities and the part they have played in history. Seeing it all, as every great historian must, *sub specie æternitatis*, he finds that it is by minorities that the great things—the worthwhile things and the greatly evil things too—have been achieved. And of effective minorities he finds there are two kinds, the *dominant* and the *creative*. In each we find energy, intensity of purpose and the will to power; whilst all majorities are marked by confused thinking, inertia, divided purposes and lack of staying power. Thus they render themselves the tools and servants of minority groups whose intrinsic strength is not comparable to that of the potential strength of the majorities they dominate. Just such a dominant minority was the group, with Adolf Hitler as their leader, mouthpiece and symbol, which in 1933 secured control over the German people and for twelve years held them in bemused servitude. Just so did Mussolini and his myrmidons hold the Italian people in thrall, for even longer. Each was a dominant minority—coarse, self-assertive, glittering, sterile, as such minorities are doomed to be.

So, too, though in a very different way, have the British for a while been a dominant minority in South Africa. Conquest and occupation, first in 1806 and then nearly a century later in 1902, established them as just such a minority. It was a position that in the nature of things could not endure; and it has passed.

What remains, then, for South Africans of English stock? Are they to sever the ties which bind them to England or Scotland, and make no attempt to pass these things on to their children? To watch these latter absorbed and assimilated into Afrikanerdom? Or, holding on to the English heritage, must they become aliens in the land of their birth?

No, that—*Laus Deo*—is not the alternative before the English South African. For there is also a minority that does not seek to dominate—that *creative* minority which Professor Toynbee sees at work in history. It is a minority which sets little store by self-consciousness, and is thereby distinguished from all ' nationalisms.' Its leaders have to be content to forgo place and power and office. There must be in them a single-hearted devotion to all that is ' universal,' and not merely local in the tradition they have inherited. Of this tradition they must be the guardians, in the midst of a majority most of whom neither understand nor value these things, and they have to show all the self-discipline and self-denial that this demands. And the test of a creative minority, be it remembered, is its capacity to provoke and stimulate the best elements in the majority to imitate it—its way of life and thought, its studies and habits and clothes and games.

Such a creative minority English South Africans can yet become, if they will and are prepared to pay the price. There is no need, on awakening to the reality that dominance has gone, to suppose that the alternative before them is that of absorption. Their numbers alone make that impossible. So do the strength and the quality of the tradition and heritage they represent and for which they stand. So, be it said with all modesty, does the quality of their own work and of the part they play in the life of the Union. Much depends on their present leaders. They need great patience and great courage. Not for them are the prestige and dignities and emoluments of office. To them politics must mean the political desert; yet they must not eschew politics. From the desert, let them recall, the best and noblest things have often come. They are the guardians of that which South Africa greatly needs to-day. Her children will need it no less in the years ahead.

RONALD FAIRBRIDGE CURREY

Son of H. L. Currey, at one time Private Secretary to Cecil Rhodes and a member of the last Cape Ministry before Union. Educated at St. Andrew's College, Grahamstown; Rhodes University College, Grahamstown; and Trinity College, Oxford. Rhodes Scholar, 1912. Served in first World War in 4th Black Watch; awarded Military Cross, 1916; Bar to Military Cross, 1917. Joint Headmaster of Ridge Preparatory School, Johannesburg, 1927-30; Rector of Michaelhouse, 1930-38; Headmaster of St. Andrew's College, Grahamstown, since 1939.

CHAPTER IV

The South African Jewish Community

PHYLLIS LEWSEN

IN 1841, seventeen Jews came to pray together in Cape Town on the Eve of the Day of Atonement. This was the first Jewish congregation, and the beginnings of Jewish community life in South Africa. Centuries before, however, Jews had played their individual roles in South African history. In the Portuguese Era of Exploration there were Jewish sailors and interpreters with the fleets, and Jewish cartographers and astrologers prepared maps and instruments for the great voyages.[1] In the next century, Jews in the Netherlands, many of them refugees from Portuguese oppression, helped to establish the Dutch spice trade. There were Jews associated with the Dutch East India Company, even, on occasions, in the Supreme 'Council of Seventeen'; but in the Company's possession religious uniformity was imposed, so that during its regime (1652-1797) there were no practising Jews at the Cape. Jewish names do appear on the 17th and 18th century Cape burgher rolls, but they are those of concealed or converted Jews who have left no Jewish descendants.

The Batavian administration (1803-6) first introduced the principle of religious toleration to the Cape. This was maintained, after 1806, by the British administration; and a small Jewish immigration, mainly from Britain and the German States, began. Nineteen Jews, for example, came out with the 1820 British settlers. Until the discovery of diamonds, however, there were few Jews, because there was little immigration of any kind to South Africa.[2] In these early years there were also quite frequent conversions, so that a number of the pioneer Jewish

---

[1] Two Jews sailed with da Gama on his first voyage to India.
[2] The Kimberley synagogue, built at the 'Diamond Fields' in 1876 was the third in South Africa.

families have been entirely absorbed into the English and Afrikaans communities.[1]

Though the community was so small, the early Jewish economic contribution was considerable. The introduction of the merino sheep to the Cape (Maximilian Thalwitzer, 1841), of cotton and the hardy Uba sugar-cane to Natal (Jonas Bergtheil and Daniel de Pass), the importation of angora goats from Turkey to start the mohair industry (the Mosenthals), the beginnings of a coastal shipping service (the de Pass brothers), the development of the ostrich feather industry (the Mosenthals again), are all the work of creative Jewish economic pioneers.

It was the obscure Jewish trader, however, who provided the characteristic economic contribution; Jewish produce merchants and country store-keepers, and the pedlars who got so warm a welcome from the isolated inland farmers with whom they traded, all served an indispensable function in an undeveloped country. They brought a market to the farmer, thereby giving value to his produce; and at the same time they brought him the goods he needed.. 'The small trader,' says the economist Professor Hutt, ' has played an immensely important role in this country. He has been the efficient link between a backward back-veld and a progressive outer world. He has brought an apathetic . . . community of farmers into touch with an eager industrial and mining class to their mutual benefit.'[2]

The latter part of this process began with the economic expansion caused by diamonds and gold. There were Jews, of course, among the Kimberley diamond magnates, and the capitalists who developed the Johannesburg gold-mining industry. Their emergence, however, is an individual success-phenomenon, and to this day mining in South Africa is not ' Jewish controlled.' Most of the Jews who came to Kimberley in the seventies were traders and shopkeepers; those who came in the eighties and nineties, after the gold developments, were mainly 'foreign' Jews from Eastern Europe, who for generations had been excluded from other economic activities. Fortunately, they fitted easily and productively into the expanding South African

[1] For example, Saul Solomon, the distinguished Parliamentarian; and Frans and Jan Lion Cachet (noted for their work for the Afrikaans language and the Dutch Reformed Church).

[2] *S.A. Journal of Economics*, pp. 281–90.

economy. In the towns there was no conflict with the English commercial and mining classes, for there was room enough for all. In the country, relations with the Afrikaner farmers were good; in fact Jews often found it easier to establish personal contacts with them than with the more formal British. But the picture of Jewish status among the Boers in general as the beloved ' people of the Book ' is a romantic projection. Wherever Jews came together in sufficient numbers, they tended to form a cohesive social group, bound together by the practice of their religion, and by their pattern of communal and family life. The individual immigrant—a stranger struggling to adapt himself to a new country—found psychological security in his membership of this group. At the same time he was clearly eager to become a South African, anxious to give his children every possible opportunity of South African education—in short, to ' assimilate ' in everything save religion and group identity.

This Eastern European immigration is by far the most important Jewish influence on the South African Jewish community. It was set off in the 1880's by Czarist persecutions, which drove a million Jews, in twenty-five years, from the huddled ghettoes of Eastern Europe. An eddy of this wave, mainly from a few small towns and villages, was what reached South Africa. The general pattern was as follows : the new immigrant, delighted with the spaciousness and freedom of South African life, would send his first savings to bring out his family and friends. The ' griener ' (green ones—foreigners) were met at the docks, fed, housed and often started off with a loan and much good advice by their relatives or their ' landsleit ' (fellow-townsmen). In their turn they too sent back their savings. All over South Africa new communities grew up and new congregations were established, mainly and sometimes entirely consisting of Eastern European Jews.

There were two other peaks of immigration, after the South African War and in the nineteen-twenties; and the influx from Eastern Europe only dried up when the Union Government passed its Immigration (Quota) Act of 1930. After 1932 there was for a short while a new influx of highly westernized Jews, escaping from Hitler's Germany, till the problem of their ' assimilability ' in its turn provoked the Aliens Act of 1937. About

12,000 German Jews came in altogether. To-day there is no Jewish immigration of any importance. The challenge and stimulus of absorbing new immigrants from the older Jewish communities is over and even the cultural influence of European Jewry is at an end, for the parent communities have been destroyed.

There were, in 1946, 103,435 Jews in South Africa, forming approximately 4·4 per cent of the European population. The great majority were born in South Africa. They live mainly in the cities and large towns—about 50,000 live in Johannesburg, where they are spread out to-day among the professions and in secondary industry, as well as in trade and commerce.[1] There is a very small and, individually, very enterprising Jewish farming segment.[2] On the other hand, the Jewish village and small-town communities have dwindled in some places to nothing. The reasons are mostly sociological ones—for example, the desire to keep the family together as the younger generation move to the cities. But the impact of anti-Semitic movements and tendencies cannot be ignored.

Political anti-Semitism is not indigenous to South Africa—the influence of Nazi propaganda and funds has been clearly traced. But it appeared at a time when Jews, horrified at what was happening in Germany, were particularly sensitive to its manifestations. Jews who stayed on in the country remained, very often, on the most cordial terms with their neighbours. Others felt, rightly or wrongly, that there was ' no future ' for them in a hostile, or potentially hostile, environment; and this was one of their reasons for moving. This impaired feeling of security is certainly present in the city as well, but the individual Jew feels less exposed to anti-Semitism, and can more easily avoid it.[3]

Jews share actively in every phase of South African life; so that to single out the eminent Jewish writers or artists, for example, is to this extent misleading : their work stems from their South African environment, and in its turn is part of the South

[1] Secondary industry in South Africa is the term applied to industry other than mining or agriculture. The Jews have been particularly enterprising in its establishment.

[2] E.g. pioneers in citrus and deciduous fruit farming, the late ' mealie-king,' the ' potato-king ' and the ' ostrich-feather king.'

[3] Either by mixing in tolerant circles or by belonging to an exclusively Jewish social group.

African culture. Sarah Gertrude Millin, who is Jewish, is South Africa's most famous novelist. Moses Kottler and Lippy Lipshitz are eminent South African sculptors; that they are Jews is not irrelevant to their work, but does not determine the nature of their contribution. As a group, Jews are particularly active as patrons of art and music. In language they belong mainly to the English-speaking section; because they are city-dwellers, not because they are unsympathetic to Afrikaans cultural aspirations. In party politics there are no specific Jewish attitudes—unless a party group chooses to provoke these by preaching political anti-Semitism, or has avowed anti-Semites among its leaders. Both were the case in the Nationalist Party when it was in Opposition, particularly during the war years. Since its coming into power no anti-Semitic measures have been mooted, and the Prime Minister has disclaimed anti-Semitism as a policy. The Nationalist Party in the Transvaal does not, however, admit Jewish members; and this, and the party's past record, must greatly have reduced its proportion of Jewish votes.

Jewish responses to the Native problem and the Coloured problem are also characteristically South African. That is to say, the great majority believe in segregation and have strong social prejudices against non-Europeans. Those who do not, form part of a small minority drawn from all groups. The difference in viewpoint between a Jewish conservative and a Jewish liberal on such topics as academic segregation for non-Europeans, or the proper handling of Native labour, would very aptly illustrate the extremes to be found in South African colour attitudes.

Jews do, however, often show a specifically Jewish reaction to overseas politics. At all times and in all places they respond sharply to the sufferings of fellow-Jews in other lands. Where a country's Jewish policies are neutral or tolerant, South African Jews share the attitudes which they glean from South African newspapers and political speeches. But if anti-Semitism or anti-Zionism is manifest, or even suspected, they react with quick hostility.[1] The South African Jewish press keeps its readers in-

---

[1] There was considerable anti-British feeling after the last war, and also during the Israel-Arab war, because of British Palestine policy. This seems now to be abating.

formed about Jewish news all over the world. The two leading newspapers, the *Zionist Record* and the *South African Jewish Times,* have a very wide circulation; and a great deal of influence on their readers' overseas political attitudes.

For all they have in common with other South Africans, most South African Jews feel, in addition, a positive Jewish group feeling, and join in a distinctive Jewish community life. If pressed to a definition of their Jewishness they might specify religion, or the fact that they are 'more at home' with Jews socially; in addition, many would claim a sense of Jewish national identity, similar to that of the Afrikaans South African group, but in no way conflicting with their loyalty as South African citizens. The fringe of 'marginal' or 'assimilated' Jews is drawn into the Jewish community at times of crisis.

To deal first with the religious element: there are two Jewish denominations in South Africa, the Orthodox and the Reform. The latter was started in 1933 with four members, and has now five temples and 5,000 adherents. Its expansion does not, however, seem to have been at the expense of the Orthodox congregations, which have also increased in numbers, and in general show more vitality than they did fifteen years ago. The main differences between the two are in ritual and synagogue organization. The Orthodox synagogue observes the ancient traditional services and customs, including the segregation of women—a symbol of inferiority which has no counterpart in modern Jewish social life. In the Reform temple the service has been modernized, and a proportion of the prayers are in English. Classes in Hebrew and in the Jewish religion are an important function of both types of congregation, and in recent years nursery schools and adult study classes have been added.

There is a core of the devout in every synagogue as in every church, but on the whole South African Jews of to-day would not claim to be a strongly religious group. They are reluctant, however, to abandon all Jewish religious traditions. The Sabbath and the dietary laws may not be rigorously observed except by a minority; but the Barmitzvah (confirmation of boys at their thirteenth birthday) is celebrated even in the most secularized Jewish families, and most Jewish children receive some instruction in Hebrew and in Jewish history.[1] For three days a year synagogues are crowded for the High Festivals, when members do more than just formally attend, but are absorbed for the moment into a living congregation. A surprising interest is taken, too, in the conduct of synagogue affairs. The motive seems often more communal than religious. Something of the wider significance of the synagogue in the Middle Ages, when it was in the fullest sense a community centre as well as a house of prayer, seems to have continued into modern Jewish South African life.

Another communal influence, similar in historical origin, is the responsibility that Jews continue to feel for the poorer members of their community. It is an unspoken axiom that Jews must care for their own charities, so much so that the ' Chevra Kadisha ' (Burial and Philanthropic Society) was often established even before the religious congregation. The ' Chevra Kadisha ' still flourishes in every Jewish community together with a host of benevolent societies, all maintained by voluntary contributions, and run by energetic committees elected from the men and women of position, wealth and social responsibility in the community.[2]

Another trait which is part of the Jewish social inheritance is the strong Jewish family feeling, extending to quite remote members of the clan. It is responsible for the dynastic element which enters into almost every Jewish marriage, however humble. Thirty or forty years ago, Jewish society was stratified according to the immigrants' place of birth. The Polish, Lithuanian, German and Baltic Jews formed distinct social groups, and a marriage across these, between a ' German ' and a ' Litvak,' for example, would very often cause family heartburning. To-day such divisions are largely smudged out; but when it comes to ' mixed ' marriages with Gentiles, it is family sentiment as often as religious conviction that is decisive in preventing them.

Jewish anxieties about anti-Semitism, and their effect in

---

[1] There has been a considerable increase in Hebrew studies since Hebrew became a living language in Palestine.

[2] On the Witwatersrand a Jewish welfare council co-ordinates the activities of at least ten important philanthropic societies, employs trained social workers, and follows the methods of family rehabilitation rather than charity.

stimulating group feeling, have already been noted. Though all Jews are sensitive to anti-Semitism, the individual response varies greatly. Some are indifferent to its minor manifestations; others are excessively sensitive, always on guard in non-Jewish society, and greatly distressed, for example, if there is public criticism of individual Jews. The corrective for this state of mind is more, and not less, contact with members of other groups. But this is not always easy in South Africa, where the prevailing (and growing) tendency is to exaggerate the value of group life and to accentuate differences rather than similarities.

This latter is the negative side of Jewish group life. Its positive side is shown by the vigour and variety of Jewish communal activities. The South African Jewish Board of Deputies, whose task it is to represent Jewish organizations officially (and to some extent to co-ordinate their activities), to-day includes 304 affiliated societies. Its official philosophy is that of ' cultural pluralism ' : to encourage Jews ' to live as free and equal citizens (of South Africa), integrated into the framework of South African national life, and simultaneously maintaining our own group life.'[1] The Board is always on the watch for any challenge to Jewish citizen rights. It acts as spokesman for the Jews on public or controversial occasions, and is the accepted liaison between the Jewish community and the Government. It does not, however, represent individual Jews except through the affiliated organizations—it is not a Jewish parliament—and its influence over Jews is therefore mainly advisory.

To indicate the range of communal activity and interests, these are some of the societies that collaborate with the Board of Deputies : the network of Jewish educational institutions, including afternoon, nursery and a few day schools; the Ort-Oze (7,000 members), which encourages Jews to enter skilled occupations in the trades and agriculture; the Hebrew Order of David (twenty lodges), which works mainly as a sick benefit and general social insurance society; and the Union of Jewish Women, with a similar outlook to the Board of Deputies.[2] Clubs such as the

[1] Saron, *The Revolution in Jewish Life*.
[2] The Union of Jewish Women (forty-three branches, fourteen outposts) engages in non-European welfare work in the larger cities, and sponsors a students' hostel and a parasitology laboratory in Jerusalem.

Jewish Guild and the Durban Jewish Club have a primarily social function.[1] Sports clubs, like Balfour Park, are partly a deliberate assertion of Jewish group life, partly a response to the exclusive Gentile sporting club.[2] Then there are the Yiddish cultural societies, the dramatic and musical groups, the numerous benevolent and helping hand societies; and besides all these, overlapping into every phase of organized Jewish life, the host of Zionist societies, representing the most important influence of all in Jewish group and community life.

Zionism, in its simplest definition, is the desire to assist in the upbuilding of the Jewish National Home in Israel. It has always been strong in South Africa, particularly among the Lithuanian immigrants, some of whom had belonged to foundation Zionist societies in Europe. Within a year of the first World Zionist Conference at Basle in 1897, there were nine Zionist societies on the Witwatersrand. Since the Nazi persecutions, and even more so since the war—with its extermination of six million Jews in Europe—Zionism has grown enormously in numbers and influence. The establishment of the State of Israel, and the Israel-Arab war, brought still more supporters; while since the peace the responsibility of the Zionist Movement abroad for helping settle displaced persons and refugees in Israel has maintained the pitch of Zionist effort and enthusiasm. The South African Zionist Federation to-day comprises approximately 375 constituent societies, including eighty-seven youth societies. Women members alone total 15,000 while in the last elections for the World Zionist Congress, 29,011 votes were cast in South Africa. These are astonishing figures when one considers the total Jewish population of the Union (103,435 Jews). On the other hand, ' Zionists ' range from sympathizers whose motives are mainly philanthropic or cultural, to the ardent Jewish nationalists, whose Zionist work engrosses almost all their leisure.

---

[1] These clubs provided meals, lodging and recreation for thousands of soldiers of all denominations during the war.

[2] Balfour Park, however, admits non-Jewish members. Another response to ' Gentile ' exclusiveness in sport is the club founded by Jews, but then run as a general club. 37.8 per cent of 318 people who filled in an attitude questionnaire form preferred a Jewish to a general sports club, giving such reasons as : ' They don't want us ' ; ' Feel more at home with your own people ' ; and ' No anti-Semitism.'

However, only about a thousand South African Jews have so far settled in Israel.

The strength of the Zionist Movement in South Africa is due partly to world political tendencies; partly to South Africa's own ideological climate, with its strong encouragement of separate group life.[1] The general influences of Zionism on the South African Jewish community has been to replace and reinforce the earlier communal solidarity based on religious unity. There is no denying that the traditional Jewish religious culture has waned. In a secular age religion is an individual rather than a group phenomenon, and has not the same power as a secular national movement to generate the emotions which bind a group together.

This chapter is an analysis of the South African Jewish community at a special moment of time. Since Hitler came into power this community has been exposed to a constant series of shocks; emotionally it is therefore at a particularly high pitch, and its future direction and development cannot be anticipated. A great deal will depend on the political and social pattern in South Africa, and a great deal also on the nature of the influence emanating from Israel. It is on a synthesis between these and its own past that the future of the South African Jewish community will depend.

PHYLLIS LEWSEN

Mrs. Phyllis Lewsen was born in 1916 on a farm in the Transvaal. She graduated at the Witwatersrand University, taking the M.A. degree in History in 1940.

Mrs. Lewsen has lectured in English and History at the Witwatersrand University. A monograph on Cape Colony constitutional development in the 19th century was published in 1942 in the *Archives Year Book for South African History*. She is at present engaged on a biographical study of a leading South African statesman (1842-1926). Her research has all been on general 19th and 20th century South African History, and this is the first specifically Jewish theme on which she has written.

---

[1] Leaders of both the United and Nationalist Parties have many times expressed their sympathy with Zionism, and the South African Government was one of the first to give *de jure* recognition to the State of Israel.

With a family of young children, and her research and lecturing work to keep her busy, Mrs. Lewsen finds little time for committee work of any description. She is much interested, however, in Adult Education, and has given a number of lecture courses on South African History to the South African Institute of Citizenship.

CHAPTER V

The Bantu Peoples

SELBY BANGANI NGCOBO

THE word ' Bantu,' meaning ' People,' is a name that occurs in all the languages of the Native tribes that inhabit the south-eastern parts of Africa. To-day the word ' Bantu ' has been adopted by the Europeans to represent those Native languages that have a fundamentally common grammatical morphology. With the Native tribes themselves, however, the name ' Bantu,' as will presently be shown, has more than a purely linguistic significance.

What may be regarded as the history of the Bantu comes from two sources : (a) the myths, legends and oral history of the different Bantu groups, handed down orally from generation to generation; and (b) the ethnological accounts furnished mainly by European scholars. There is very little that is reliable and enlightening in Bantu oral histories once they have been shorn of what is merely boastful, fanciful and legendary. Such history has nevertheless served to furnish interesting clues upon which European scholars have produced a historical synthesis based partly on evidence from Bantu languages themselves, partly on archæological or anthropological data and on verifiable or verified events in recorded history.

The cradle of the Bantu is believed to be Central Africa, in particular the area of the upper waters of the Congo in the west, the upper Nile in the north, and the Great African Lakes in the eastern part of Africa.[1] At about the time of the 6th century A.D. the Bantu began to migrate southwards. At that time they were a people possessing some strength of numbers, agricultural knowledge, mining skill, implement-manufacturing

---

[1] Schapera, *The Bantu-speaking Tribes of South Africa*, pp. 6-8.

ability and political organization. But even then the Bantu were not a pure negroid race, having mixed their blood with peoples of other stock such as the North African tribes and the Arabs.

According to Father Bryant,[1] the Bantu in their southward march crossed the upper Zambezi in strength without the use of canoes. Thereafter the Herero separated themselves off to go and settle in what is now South-West Africa. The rest of the Bantu slowly pushed on until they reached the upper waters of the Limpopo. But by that time some of the tribal aggregations had settled in the area between the Zambezi and Limpopo rivers, and further, the advanced Bantu groups had come into contact with the Bushman, from whom they picked up the clicks in their language. Bryant states that upon reaching the upper Limpopo the Bantu separated—the Sotho group in different waves tending to move down along the centre of Southern Africa, while the Nguni and Shangana-Tongo groups turned towards the east coast. Between 1500 and 1700 these latter groups, in waves of different strength, moved down along the East African coast, and, in the process, occupying areas which are now known as Portuguese East Africa, Zululand, Natal, the Transkei and the eastern parts of the Cape Province.

Dr. van Warmelo,[2] the present Government ethnologist, regards all this as speculation or intelligent guessing. He points out that the above facts cannot be verified from Native tradition because it is weak in chronology and scanty in regard to truth; it is still not clear where the various migrations began, what routes were followed and what were the experiences of one group with another. Much that is vital in the history, language and culture of the Bantu still remains to be accounted for.

Ethnic and Linguistic Groups

Having given a brief and cursory account of the history of the Bantu, it is now necessary to classify them on the basis of what is known of their linguistic and ethnological characteristics. For the sake of easy reference mention will also be made of the different geographical regions which various Bantu groups occupy.

[1] A. T. Bryant, *Olden Times in Zululand and Natal*, Chap. I.
[2] Schapera, *The Bantu-speaking Tribes of South Africa*, Chap. III.

The main divisions of the Southern Bantu are as follows[1] :

1. Western, spreading north and south of the Okavango river and including the Ambo, the Herero and the Mbudu people.

2. South-central, comprising the Shona tribes of Southern Rhodesia.

3. South-eastern, situated principally in the Union of South Africa, but also extending into Bechuanaland and the head-waters of the Zambezi. This sub-division includes the following groups or clusters of tribes :

(a) The Nguni group, comprising the Xhosa, Tembu, Fingo, Pondo, Zulu and Swazi tribes, all of whom inhabit the area lying between the Drakensberg mountains and the sea, and stretching from Swaziland to the Ciskei in the Cape Province; the languages spoken by these tribes have clicks.

(b) The Shangana-Tonga group, most of whom live in Portuguese East Africa; sections of these people are now to be found in Northern Zululand and in the north-eastern Transvaal. These people have no clicks in their language.

(c) The Sotho group, comprising the Basuto of Basutoland, the Bapedi in the north and north-eastern Transvaal and the Bechuana or Tswana along the western borders of the Transvaal.

(d) The Venda group in the north-eastern Transvaal; the culture of these people is very distinctive.

The subsequent account will be confined entirely to those Bantu groups that are to be found within the borders of the Union of South Africa. The aggregations of tribes contained within each group have cultures which show some marked re-semblances. On account of wars of conquest and extermination, migrations and European influences, it is not possible to delimit exactly the area of one tribe from that of another. As between the main Bantu groups, there are certain broad similarities and dissimilarities.[2] Among all groups the kinship structure is found with its emphasis on seniority and deference to rank and status. Though the maternal connection is more emphasized by certain

---

[1] Schapera, *The Bantu-speaking Tribes of South Africa*, p. 23.
[2] Schapera, *The Bantu-speaking Tribes of South Africa*, Chap. IV.

tribes, patrilineal descent is observed by all. Polygamy is practised by all Bantu groups and *lobola*[1] is necessary to a valid
marriage; among all groups there is a political structure which
centres round the members of a ruling clan or tribe. Land is
everywhere communally held. Ancestor worship is practised by
all Bantu.

The broad dissimilarities are in respect of historical background, mode of settlement, kraal organization, marriage practices, and social structure or organization. The Nguni peoples
prohibit parallel and cross-cousin marriage, whereas the Sotho
peoples allow it; the Sotho are totemistic, but the Nguni are not;
the ' cattle complex ' is very pronounced among the Nguni, but
circumcision is relatively unimportant. The Sotho accord a different status to each wife in a polygamous household, but they
do not divide the kraal into sections as do the Nguni.[2]

The patriotism of the tribes that make up the main groups is
local or regional. It expresses itself as love of the mountains and
the rivers of the inhabited area, pride in one's people, their language, customs and traditions, loyalty to the chief, and a readi-
ness to defend and die for the ancestral lands. Evidence of this
patriotism of the Bantu is to be found in their ordinary conversation and in the praises of their chiefs and their genealogy.

Each of the Bantu groups refers to itself as ' the People,' i.e.,
' Abantu ' in Nguni or ' Batho ' in Sotho. Among Caucasian,
Semitic and Mongolian people are to be found the same ideas of
being the elect of humanity.

This sense of importance or racial pride expresses itself differently in each tribal group. The Zulus, for example, are more
forthright in calling other tribes ' animals ' and only themselves
' the People '; the Xhosas are said to adopt a haughty attitude
and patronizing manner towards non-Xhosa persons. The Sotho,
on the other hand, use derogatory terms to convey the idea that
persons who are not Sotho by birth are less than human and may
therefore be despised. Thus, both among the Nguni and Sotho
groups outsiders or strangers have been regarded as inferior or as

---

[1] Compensation for the loss of a daughter. Among pastoral tribes this consists
of cattle. Besides compensation it is a form of insurance for the good treatment
of the daughter. It is the act legalizing marriage.
[2] H. P. Junod, *Bantu Heritage*, p. 22.

belonging to a lower order of humanity. No doubt the same sentiments are to be found among the Shangana-Tonga and the Venda groups.

Closer contacts between the various tribes at school, in labour districts, in urban areas, and the effect of inter-marriage have had the result of modifying the unfavourable attitudes and views about people of other tribes. To-day it is becoming more and more the practice for members of different tribes to refer to each other according to the respective and respectable tribal names. While it is still true that in unguarded moments or in a fit of anger one person may refer to a person of another tribe as an ' animal ' or in some other derogatory term, yet such expressions are avoided in public speech and in polite conversation. Further, Bantu nationalism is reinforcing the tendency to mutual respect among members of different tribes.

An idea of the kind of people the Bantu wish to be may be obtained by considering answers to the following questions. What are the goals and objects people strive for in Bantu tribal society? What are the cultural values they uphold and cherish? What is regarded as the ideal man or woman?

Although the ideal personality type is not quite identical in all tribes, there is nevertheless a general tendency among all Bantu groups to stress certain cultural and human values as being desirable or ideal.

Firstly, the Bantu stress and value manliness, which they regard as consisting of courage and hardihood in facing difficulties, particularly physical danger. These qualities were inculcated in the veld when herding cattle and goats, in the sham fights on the veld, in the circumcision schools, and in the military kraals among the Zulus particularly.

Secondly, acumen in council, invariably held at the King's or the Chief's ' great place,' is another quality which commands respect and raises a man's stature. Men who show wisdom, discretion, and a capacity for judgment when cases or matters of state are being dealt with, become the King's or the Chief's headmen and trusted advisors. Before the establishment of European authority Bantu kings or paramount chiefs maintained a large number of courtiers who, with great dignity and decorum, conducted the affairs of the group.

Thirdly, firmness and dignity is another highly-valued personality trait. These are best exemplified in the person of the
patriarchal head or the kraal (village) head. The kraal head has
complete jurisdiction over all property and all persons within the
village; he is the authority who gives orders which must be
obeyed; he is responsible for the behaviour of the members of the
village since all these persons bear his name, and an evil deed
done by a single member of his family reflects adversely on him,
while every honourable act redounds to his credit. The nature
of his wisdom and authority therefore is to a large extent
reflected in the personalities of his wives and children.

Fourthly, generosity and consideration for the needs, feelings
and welfare of others, particularly the less fortunate, are regarded
as the hallmark of a good or a great man. Such a man always
welcomes and entertains strangers and travellers, and harbours the
waifs and strays of society. Every great man—a man having
several wives, a large herd of cattle and other stock, several fields
and many huts—is expected to keep an open house, a sort of
free-for-all who care to come. The advantage of a polygamous
kraal is that it allows for the display of munificence. It is most
damaging to a man's reputation to accuse him of having denied
others food, meat, beer and accommodation when he had these.

Fifthly, the Bantu attach great importance to the principle of
reciprocity upon which their life is based. The Bantu as a whole
are highly co-operative, and as E. J. and J. D. Krige have expressed it, ' participation in the benefits of the culture depends
upon not offending against the reciprocities.' And (we are still
quoting the Kriges) ' the reciprocities are not precisely calculated
equivalences, nor a series of exactly-balanced obligations. People
do not consciously think of the long-run result of their behaviour,
and they know that social duty done is not always sure of
reward. Hard as the axe chops, it cannot eat the honey it ex-
tracts, say the Lovedu, to warn those who expect that their
effort will inevitably be rewarded.'

It is this principle which explains all such co-operative efforts
as ' amalimo,' i.e., co-operative farming activities, and to a series
of ' gifts of exchange ' which are all a feature of Bantu life. The
delinquent who offends against this principle and does not join in
the co-operative life may find himself without any help when he

most needs it. Hence fear of isolation and helplessness act as a sufficient deterrent to unco-operative behaviour and to greed and miserliness.

A good woman or one that everybody admires is one who is industrious and obedient. As we have indicated, the woman in the home is there to serve her husband; and she fails in her duties if she does not respect him, respect his parents and his ancestral gods. Such a woman calls the anger of the ancestral gods on her head in particular and on the family in general. In their anger the gods or the ancestors may strike the children with disease, or many curses may come to the home through her disobedience. The gods are very fickle and easily moved to anger, and malicious talk and noise in the home are some of the major causes of their anger. A woman who talks too much and is very quarrelsome is therefore not a blessing! Then also she must be industrious, for the rounds of feasts and beer-drinking in particular are dependent on the stores that are in the home. It is her job to see that the fields are planted with corn and to gather it in to the garners. A bad woman, therefore, is argumentative, obstinate, lazy, or a slovenly worker.

Individuals whose life is still tribally orientated seek to conform to the ideals that have been analysed above. Among the Bantu who have been educated or Christianized, the ideal personality aimed at is that of a civilized man or woman or a Christian saint as the case may be; but the extent to which truly Christian ethics and ideals move even those Bantu who are regular churchgoers may be doubted.

Those members of the Bantu group who have acquired political consciousness have also begun to desire and work for national unity of all Bantu tribes, and to attain to a position within the body politic where they can be citizens and no longer the wards of the European population. Such, then, are the ideas of the Bantu as to themselves, as a people in the past, now, and in the future.

In the ethnological accounts of Bantu life that are generally current, much emphasis is laid on the co-operative life of the Bantu—corporate living in the kraal, corporate ceremonies and festivals, corporate obligations and legal responsibilities of the kraal head. The impression has then been conveyed that indi-

PLATE VI

A Typical Zulu Kraal in Northern Zululand.
It is built in horseshoe shape, with a cattle kraal in the centre.

[To face page 54.

PLATE VII

A. GIRAFFE IN THE KRUGER NATIONAL PARK.

B. SUGAR GROWING IN NATAL.
Drought is a constant threat in this area. The irrigation channel in this pictur
follows the contour above the narrow-gauge railway.

viduality is denied or given no scope in Bantu society. This is not so. The Bantu certainly have never held the view that all persons must be identical or exactly alike; they recognize human variability and differentiate people into various psychological types.

Individuality does have scope for expressing itself in dress, in arts and crafts, and in games and ceremonies where there are no set rules and no set actors. Since a man with an engaging personality is likely to be much more successful than a man without such a personality, much care and thought was, and still is, being given to the development of personality through the use and aids of medicinal fats, drugs and herbs. In combat, success goes to the man who is not only brave and strong but adopts tactical skill in the using of the shield, the spear and sticks; in the hunt, too, individual skill is regarded as an asset; in dances and games, individuals with initiative and resourcefulness often introduce variations that win the admiration and praise of their onlookers. Whilst everybody conforms to the general pattern, within that pattern individual variation was, and is, allowed.

Since only those belonging to one's group can be regarded as a human being and be part of the ' Bantu ' or ' Batho,' it is not surprising that the Europeans who came to Southern Africa were not referred to as ' people ' (abantu). Indeed new names were invented or coined to express either the peculiar physical features of the Europeans or their different ways, dress and manner of living.

The Zulus referred to the Europeans as ' Abandlebe Zikhanya Ilanga,' meaning ' those whose ears reflect the sunlight '; sometimes they were called ' Abalumbi ' (magicians), a compliment, no doubt, to the white man's technical skill and knowledge. The Sotho referred to the Europeans as ' Mokhako,' i.e., those having the colour of a yellowish claypot. At times even more uncomplimentary or derogatory terms and expressions were used.

To-day, on account of the prestige of the White people as conquerors and a governing race, the Bantu have thought it prudent to use such neutral words as ' Abelungu ' in Zulu-Xhosa languages or ' Makhooa ' in Sotho languages, when referring to the White people. Nowadays the Zulus, for example, speak of the Europeans simply as ' Abamhlope,' i.e., the Whites.

The Bantu readily admit the superiority of European arms, technical skill and knowledge; they also admit that the materials of European culture are better and more convenient than most of what they have. But at the same time they reject much of the morality, folk-ways and habits of the Europeans, and claim that their code of behaviour and morals are better. To the Bantu the Europeans, probably because of their materialistic outlook, lack the essential quality of human beings, which is best conveyed by the Zulu word ' Ubuntu.'

The different groups live so closely in South African life that, despite the general attitudes as given above, there very often develop personal friendships which are uninfluenced by the general attitudes of the different racial groups. Thus we find Bantu-Indian friendships which are as intimate and as cordial as family ties. Such relations exist also between Bantu and Coloured, although Bantu-Coloured cordiality does not, in the Bantu mind, seem to warrant special notice and comment, for some Coloured persons are part of the Bantu group, whilst others do not touch Bantu life so as to cause resentment.

Personal relations between Bantu and Europeans are common and can be very intimate. But, let us add, they are very uneasy and rest on an unsure foundation. The friendship is made difficult by the fact that a European friend is and can only be a friend (with few exceptions) away from his friends and family. If he takes a Bantu friend to his house, very often he runs the risk of driving away some of his European friends, and if not that, then his Bantu friend will have to be subjected in his friend's house to a number of insults such as being called ' Boy ' or ' John ' or some such other name by the white friends of the European.

Another bar to real friendship between Bantu and European in South Africa is the fact that the cultural differences are very marked. A tribal African cannot really be friendly with a European, for the basis on which a friendship should rest is lacking. There is no compatibility of interests or tastes, and the disparity in the cultural level (in the æsthetic sense) is unbridgeable. Bantu-European friendships develop and are maintained, however, between university students and on the high academic levels, where the Bantu have reached a sufficiently high level of culture to meet on equal terms with Europeans. Further, within the framework of master and servant relationships there are numerous cases of friendship between the Bantu and Europeans, whether as householders, artisans, foremen and owners of businesses.

In the field of race relations in general the Bantu make distinctions between the Jews, the Germans, the Afrikaners and the British. The Jews are regarded as being sympathetic towards the Bantu and have the reputation of being kindly and considerate employers. The Germans, probably because of their very virtues of efficiency and hard work, are regarded as hard taskmasters and strict disciplinarians.

On the whole the Bantu admire and respect the British in South Africa. British arms, which subdued the military might of the Bantu in the Cape, Basutoland, Natal and Zululand, enjoy great prestige with the Bantu; the monarchist sentiments of the British find a sympathetic chord in the Bantu with their background of kings, paramount chiefs and lesser chiefs. British missions were the first to bring to the Bantu the light of Christianity and education. The superiority of the British over the Bantu expresses itself in subtler and quieter ways. The British in the Cape Province and in Natal have been more ready to give educated Bantu suitable positions and to accord them various consideration.

The dominance of the Afrikaners is readily admitted by the Bantu, and this they ascribe to the military victories over them (the Bantu) in the last century. With the Bantu, Afrikaner republicanism has no psychological appeal whatsoever, probably because much of the Christian and educational work of the Dutch Reformed Church developed late and is mainly carried on outside the borders of the Union.

The difference in the popular views of the Bantu towards the two main sections of the European population is the result of historical circumstances, past and present relations between members of each section of the Bantu, and the outlook and views of Native policy expounded by political spokesmen from each section.

But even here some significant qualifications exist. What is said above must be looked upon as group reactions. There are many variations and deviations from the popular attitudes. It would not be correct to say that all Afrikaners hold the traditional views attributed to them as a people by the Bantu, or that there are no British people who think of the Bantu in the same terms as the traditional Afrikaners. The Bantu are aware of the courtesy and kindness of many Afrikaners, both as employers in the home and as friends in welfare work of the Church and other institutions. The master-servant bond has produced much affection during the years between Afrikaners and their employees, and where it exists its presence is an enriching factor in our relations.

Contrary to developments elsewhere in the world and in contrast to the nationalism of the Afrikaans-speaking people in the Union, Bantu nationalism has not taken the form of love of one's language and culture as represented by tribal traditions, customs and superstitions. Three reasons probably explain this. The Bantu are not a homogeneous cultural and language group, and there is therefore no movement to advance the cause of the language and culture of one Bantu group as against another. Secondly, as a dominated group the Bantu do not see any prospect whereby their languages and culture can be arrested in a national state. Thirdly, the Bantu have long suspected that the perpetuation of their languages and culture by the Government and missionaries is a means of keeping them divided and perpetuating European domination.

Bantu nationalism takes the form of love of one's people irrespective of tribal affiliations, pride in their colour, a refusal to accept ideas of inferiority, and a belief in the capacity of their people. The Bantu nationalist claims that given training and opportunity the Bantu can produce writers of note, scientists, technicians, men of learning, and artists of various sorts. As to the reasons for lack of development and inventions before contact with the Europeans, Bantu nationalists point to the diseases and deserts of the African continent, to slave exploitation, to wars and migrations, and to the fact that the African continent has few good harbours whereby other peoples from across the ocean could, until recently, have come in to stimulate and energize Africans to greater advances.

Politically, Bantu nationalism is less concerned with the

Indians and the Coloureds. It is no longer concerned with driving the Europeans out of the country. What it seeks to achieve is to abolish race discrimination which it rejects morally, and to attain legal equality and the same democratic political rights as the Europeans.

The Bantu nationalist is interested in the rise and progress of the Negroes in the United States of America because it illustrates or demonstrates to what heights on the ladder of civilization people with an essentially African background can climb in a relatively brief space of time. At the same time, the political events in India and in the Dutch East Indies are more and more receiving the attention of the Bantu nationalist. If he does not always draw exact parallels between his position and that of the Negroes, Indians and the people of the Dutch East Indies, he nevertheless draws inspiration from their more successful struggle against what has come to be regarded as political domination and oppression.

Three difficulties confront Bantu nationalism in South Africa. Firstly, the Bantu peasant masses are illiterate and lacking in political consciousness; whilst the ordinary tribesman is critical of certain European officials and of certain actions of the Government, e.g., killing of cattle or betterment schemes in the reserves, he is not yet critical of the general system of Native policy and administration; the prestige of the European overlord is still there. Secondly, the tribal differences and antipathies are still a barrier against the consummation of the national unity, i.e., the unity of all Bantu in thought, feeling and outlook. Thirdly, Bantu nationalism is discouraged by Europeans, the European Government visualizing a form of Bantu nationalism different from that advocated by Bantu nationalists.

The outside world is too foreign and too far away to interest the ordinary Bantu; occasionally he may read of war in Korea, floods in the United States of America, an earthquake in Japan, and other striking news. But since these events occur so far away they hardly concern his immediate thinking and immediate problems. Only the educated Bantu is interested in other lands and peoples, but more especially in what is happening on the continent of Africa.

The Bantu, as history books attest, have helped both the Afrikaners and the British to be established in this country. The English settlers who settled in Port Natal, Durban, in 1820 were given land and protection by Tshaka; the Bantu who lived around the port gave them labour and bartered their cattle, fowls, eggs, milk and other materials, thus enabling the Englishmen to make a living. The same was done for the Voortrekkers by the tribes living in the interior, notably by chief Moroka of Thaba 'Nchu in the Orange Free State.

True, much fighting took place in the past between the Bantu and the Europeans, much to the detriment of good race relations, but it has to be remembered that conquest over the Bantu was accomplished with the help of the Bantu as guides, auxiliaries and labourers; even during the course of the Native wars the Bantu were drawn into European society as labourers. Conflict has only interrupted an inevitable process of co-operation between Black and White.

As labourers the Bantu have contributed much to the development of the country. Matched with European capital and organizing ability they have made the roads and railways, built the villages, dorps, towns and cities; they have worked the farms and mined the gold, the diamonds and the coal. From these foundations the present political, commercial and industrial structure of the country has been built. In short, the Bantu have, at every stage, participated in the building up of Western civilization in Southern Africa.

The contribution of the Bantu to the national wealth of the country would be even greater were they not restricted in opportunities of acquiring training and working skills, and excluded from the machinery of collective bargaining as direct participants in industry. The Whites who are at the apex of the pyramid of South African civilization cannot rest secure with such a broad but weak black base.

Brief attention must now be given to the contribution of the Bantu in the field of culture as ordinarily understood.

Both the English and the Afrikaans languages have incorporated several Bantu words with rich descriptive and poetic qualities; Bantu place-names of certain localities, mountains, rivers, forests and bays have become part of the common cultural heritage.

In mission and church work the Bantu have, in several notable cases, not only helped with money, materials and labour, but they have also participated in the translation of devotional works and the Bible, and in the composition of church hymns. In this connection mention may be made of the meritorious contribution of the Rev. Tiyo Soga, Rev. John Knox Bokwe, Rev. Posselt Gumede and Mr. Ngazana Lutuli. Even where missionaries produced grammars, hymns, catechisms under their own authorship, they were nearly always assisted by Bantu converts.

In the field of general literature, encouraging developments have already taken place. As regards prose, the following books and writers have won real merit :—

Author	Book	Language
Thomas Mofolo	*Moeti oa Bochabelo,* and *Chaka*	Sesutho
S. K. Mqhoyi	*I Tyala la Mawele* (The Lawsuit of the Twins)	Xhosa
A. C. Jordan	*Ingqumbo Yeminyanya* (The Wrath of the Ancestors)	Xhosa
B. W. Vilakazi	*Noma Nini*	Zulu
J. Jolobe	*Amaro* (Essays)	Xhosa

The cause of Bantu poetry has been considerably advanced by such writings as B. W. Vilakazi's *Inkondlo ka Zulu,* S. Mqhoyi's *Imi-Hobe Nemi-Bongo,* D. C. Theko Bereng's *Lithothokiso tsa Moshoeshoe le tse Ling* (Praises of Moshesh). These efforts reveal the great possibilities that are in Bantu praises (izibongo) and epic themes. Bantu writers still fight shy of the difficult field of drama. But S. T. Plaatje's *Diphosho-phosho,* a translation into Sechuana of Shakespeare's *Comedy of Errors,* is a work of high literary merit.

General books in the vernacular now used in Bantu schools have been written by Bantu writers, mainly school teachers. The volume of such works is growing. The educated Bantu, drawing largely on the myths, legends, praises, history and traditions of their people, and employing to the full the subtleties and verse cadences in their languages, have begun to speak to themselves and to the world in the language of literature.

Whilst American Negroes have to their credit many literary

works in English, the Bantu have not yet written much in this tongue. Mention may, however, be made of D. D. T. Jabavu's *The Black Problem* (politics), Dr. S. Molema's *The Bantu* (ethnology), S. T. Plaatje's *Mhudi* (novel), R. R. Dhlomo's *An African Tragedy* (novel) and H. I. E. Dhlomo's *Nongqauze, The Girl Who Killed to Save* (drama).

Painters, particularly those depicting native scenery, have begun to emerge and to receive local recognition. But in the field of music much that is available in the vernacular is not of a high standard.

In considering Bantu Society it is not possible to speak of the family as in European society, for the simple reason that the whole social structure is differently ordered. The Bantu, for example, universally allow polygamy in their social system, and that means the family unit of father, mother and children has to be considered in relation to other social groupings of the kinship system.

The most outstanding social unit is the kraal or ' Umuzi,' which is under the control of a Headman—' *Umnumzana*.' Within it are found additional kinsmen and even unrelated individuals, who for economic reasons have attached themselves to it. Single men stay with their brothers after the death of their parents, and widows and even married women whose married lives have failed and have been ' divorced ' come to stay with their parental relatives. There are also ' borrowed ' children who belong to friends or relatives, who come to be helpful with cattle or with nursing children. Thus the number found in each kraal varies greatly according to the wealth and status of the patri-archal head.

Within the kraal, each wife with her children constitutes a family, and each family or ' *indlu* ' has its own qualified inde-pendence, with its own property which, normally, can be used only by its members, or by members of another family with its express permission. Although this is the normal thing, there are cases where the headman can, and does, requisition property from one house to be used for the benefit of another, e.g., when *lobola* has to be paid for one of the sons. When that happens, however, he is in honour bound to compensate the house so dis-possessed.

The houses in the kraal are not equal. Each takes its status from the wife occupying it, the first wife of the *umnumzana* being the principal wife. She inherits all the family heirlooms, and her house is associated with the elders of the headman's lineage. The second wife takes the next position and is often called the 'ikhohlo' or left-hand wife. The others who follow are all supporting wives to the two big houses, and are affiliated to them. The third wife, for instance, would be affiliated to the first, and the fourth to the second, and so on. The households are built according to a fairly standardized plan. Each ' *umuzi* ' has certain inevitable structures. There is the cattle kraal, which is usually in the middle, and the great house belonging to the principal wife. This is the main house in the household where important visitors are received, and where all important business of the household is transacted.

There is also the ' *ikhohlo* ' section, that is, the section of the left-hand wife with her children and dependents. Then there is the ' *ilawu* ' or bachelor's barracks. The other houses do not spring up haphazardly. They are arranged according to a definite plan so that even a stranger, on getting to the kraal, knows exactly where the principal house is or where the ' *ilawu* ' is situated.

Such, then, is the general social structure of the Nguni group.

Among the Sotho group a different social structure obtains. Instead of the characteristic household or ' *umuzi* ' found among the Nguni, there is the village among the Sotho group. These villages are generally small and occupied by people who are mostly relatives on the paternal line. Generally, however, it is not easy among the Sotho to speak of relatives on the father's side and relatives on the mother's side, because the Sotho tribes allow certain kin to marry. The general thing is cross-cousin marriage, so that, as the Kriges have put it, ' at every turn we seem to be stumbling upon the kin.'

Within these villages there are the different homesteads or families consisting of father, wife and dependent children. In a polygamous settlement each wife is entitled to her own home-stead and the wives are ranked according to their order of seniority based on the order in which they married the husband. This arrangement is altered by two conditions :

(a) If the husband later marries the girl to whom he was first engaged, or

(b) When he marries the daughter of his maternal uncle.

These two would take precedence over other wives.

These two conditions would certainly have applied in olden days. We are not sure if they still apply to-day.

A brief reference has to be made to a wider system of grouping which transcends even tribal units. This is the totem group, based on some belief by certain people that they are mystically bound together by their connection with some animal or natural object which becomes taboo to the group and an object of veneration. If it be an animal, none of that group would eat its meat or use its skin or touch it, lest some evil influence be transmitted to them by contact and thus do harm. Such an animal would not even be killed by any of the totem group.

At this stage reference may be made to the role of the family in the life of an individual, and the degree of parental authority and the form which it takes.

'The individual family in its own homestead or ' *indlu* ' is a strongly integrated group . . . and it forms through life the group with the most deep-set emotional ties and common domestic experience.'[1] It is the group which controls the more intimate social life of the people.

It is according to a certain pattern of behaviour. Where polygamy obtains, it is really a great moulding force. It determines, for instance, behaviour patterns between husbands and wives, between the co-wives and between the children of the different houses. In such a polygamous setting the relations between husbands and wives are not as intimate as they are among Europeans. The husband must be most circumspect in his relations with his wives. He must not give cause to any of them to suspect that a sister-wife is getting preferential treatment. As a result of this, he generally spends most of his time away from his wives with men, and only comes back to eat or to sleep. Under such circumstances the sort of intimacy, companionship and spiritual communion which marks the relations in European marriages is very much lacking here. This does not imply that there will be a lack of love and consideration, or that the wife might event-

[1] Schapera, *The Bantu-speaking Tribes of South Africa*, p. 75.

ually sue for a divorce on the grounds of incompatibility of interests or temperaments.

The woman, according to Bantu law, is a perpetual minor and only derives her status from that of her man. Perhaps it is much more correct to say that she can only bask in the reflected glory of her husband. A woman may, on her marriage, be given some property by her parents, but that property is really passed on to the care of her husband who is her guardian. She cannot dispose of it as she likes without prior consultation with her husband. In fact, no person can negotiate business or make a contract with a woman in Bantu society, because that would be invalid.

There is an uneasy peace between the co-wives. Although outwardly they try to appear friendly and to behave like sisters, there is a deep-seated hostility and jealousy and much malicious gossip. This thin veneer of friendliness does not deceive the children, who take their cue from their mothers and adopt their attitudes. They generally call themselves brothers and sisters, but there is always some suspicion and hostility engendered by the big question of inheritance. The children who belong to junior houses feel an acute sense of frustration. This uneasy peace and deep-seated hostility is clearly shown by the fact that the big polygamous families are always cursed with internal strife and eternal suspicions of witchcraft. Much, however, depends on the personality and wisdom of the kraal head. The kraal head has complete jurisdiction over the affairs of the kraal. His orders must be obeyed and carried out. He can dispose at will of kraal property, and even in regard to family house property he has considerable discretion. He is the representative of the inmates of the kraal, and their defender against outside interference. The religious life of the inmates is under his control and he alone can intercede with the ancestors. Hence the kraal head is treated by women and children alike with respect and veneration.

Between the father and the children there is no intimacy, and hence the father plays no direct or active part in the upbringing of the children. He is, however, always there as the ultimate sanction against bad behaviour and failure of duty.

Children are first brought up by their mothers and grandmothers who teach them respect for elders, manners, and names of things. At a later stage they are taught tribal traditions and history (story-telling) and certain virtues. Games and dancing they learn in the courtyard and there they learn to mix with other children of the kraal without friction.

From the time that a boy begins to look after goats and cattle on the veld to the time that he becomes a full adult, i.e., takes a wife, he graduates from one stage to another, and at each stage he learns certain things. Out in veld he learns botany and zoology according to Bantu ideas. In the military kraals (old days) he learnt the art of tribal warfare. In the circumcision schools he is taught about sex and the duties of a man. At each stage he is under the tutelage of his age group and has to accept its values, standards and duties. Aggregation rites mark the end of one stage and the beginning of another in life.

The girl spends most of her time with her mother and is not allowed the freedom and irresponsibility enjoyed by the boys. She learns the household arts from her mother, and by the time she is seven or eight she is fairly able to run the house, make a fire, fetch water, cook food, tend the baby and generally look after the home when the mother is out in the fields.

The question of moulding the child into an adult personality, or of giving the basic attitudes and judgments regarding the wider world, is one that is handled by the *culture*. The family, which is the society in microcosm, is naturally an important factor in calculating attitudes and values. The question cannot therefore be discussed adequately unless the whole question of growth patterns and child-rearing techniques are discussed.

The Bantu have always acknowledged the existence of a supreme being whom they referred to as ' *Unkulunkulu* ' or ' *Modimo* ' (Great One) or' *Umvelingangi* ' (the First Creator). This supreme being or High God manifests himself through thunder and lightning, and resides in heaven somewhere beyond the skies. But there, far away, ' *Unkulunkulu* ' or ' *Modimo* ' (God) remains unconcerned with what goes on on earth or in the normal affairs of life. For these reasons the Bantu have never worshipped God.

The Bantu, as still does the heathen Bantu to-day, worshipped the ancestors. According to the Bantu ideas, life is continuous, something that is carried on by the living as well as by the dead.

Beyond the grave the ancestors live the same sort of life and have the same sort of cares as they have during their ordinary physical existence. The burial and funeral rites are simply a *rite de passage* between the physical and the spiritual forms of existence. The essence of Bantu ancestor religion is very well expressed in Willoughby's phraseology, ' Bantu worship is social intercourse carried over into the spirit world.'

Elders who have died recently or in the immediate past are regarded as more responsive than those who have died in the distant past. For spiritual and material success, constant attention by way of sacrifices and offerings have to be paid to what are believed to be the needs and wishes of the ancestors. If they are neglected or their wishes disregarded, they may cause sickness to members of the kraal, sickness and loss of stock, physical injury when on a journey, and failure of the crops. Then it is the duty of the patriarchal head to intercede with the ancestral spirits. This he must do in a ceremony in the cattle kraal, but the meat and the beer reserved for the ancestors must be left at ' *emsamu*,' i.e., the end of the hut opposite the entrance. This is a sacred spot inside a hut.

In times of drought or epidemic or calamity affecting the whole tribe, the chief must make a tribal sacrifice and intercede with his royal ancestors to be benevolent towards their ' children ' (the tribe) who are still living in this mundane world. Thus the chief was, and is still, the high priest of the tribe, just as the patriarchal head is the priest of his kraal. Only the male ancestors are worshipped and, therefore, only the males can officiate in religious ceremonies.

From the very nature of their religion, it follows that the Bantu religion is localized and not portable, because it is intimately connected with the graves of the ancestors. ' It is a tribal faith anchored to the ancestral soil.' Another fact related to this is that their religion is not a worship of a single God, but a worship of a multiplicity of ' gods ' as represented in the ancestors of families, clans and tribes. Thus it is necessary when a member of a family moves away from the ancestral home, or from a clan or a tribe, as when a girl gets married, to tell the ancestors that she is going away and to ask them to extend to her their protection in her new home. Anybody who moves out of the ancestral home is like a boat cut off its moorings and, therefore, easily tossed about by the storm of life and which finally ends on the rocks. The ancestors are regarded as the guardian spirits or patron saints.

From one standpoint there is little difficulty for the Bantu in accepting Christianity, because some of the vital elements of the Christian religion are already provided for in Bantu religion, custom and law. The Bantu accept the ten commandments as being in keeping with their own ideas : self-control, brotherliness, courtesy, hospitality, and care of the weak and indigent are virtues that are continually being stressed in tribal society. The reciprocity contained in the Christian injunction ' do unto others as you would have them do unto you ' is a fundamental principle of Bantu society.

Yet the high intellectual and spiritual nature of the Christian religion, together with its formalism, is something that many Bantu groups find hard to embrace fully. There is therefore among these groups a growing tendency to hark back to the tribal ancestor-religion and to find some sort of intellectual justification in the Old Testament because it is so replete with tribal elements. These tendencies are to-day very strongly represented in the Bantu separatist churches, which are now so multifarious.

Private homes, garages, sheds, and open spaces in towns are all used as places of assembly and worship by the separatist churches. Costume, dancing and emotionalism are part of the ritual. What they lack in numbers they make up for in intense bigotry of their faith. Sacrifices and offerings are practised as the highest form of religious duty. The Bantu separatist churches therefore represent a movement away from European Christianity, European ethical conception, and European control and management, as found in the established and respectable denominations. In the rebound from these few denominations the Bantu has created a multiplicity of denominations or sects. In these sects he has the opportunity of learning the problems of organization and the handling of finances. There the lessons are being learnt slowly and with the usual mistakes. Again the separatist sects afford the Bantu an opportunity of giving free expression to his psychological nature and spiritual ideas. It remains to be seen whether, as some hope, out of their ideas and activities there will eventually arise a new Bantu religion which will be a synthesis of the true Christian spirit and the best elements of Bantu culture.

In contrast to the religious ideas of the Bantu in the reserves, and the confused doctrines of the separatists, is the relative stability of the Christian Bantu communities in the towns and in mission reserves. Here, Christian communities remain true to their European church affiliations, history, faith and doctrine.

Whereas polygamy is regarded as the ideal by followers of ancestor worship, monogamy is accepted as good by Bantu Christian communities. Sin and wrong-doing, so the heathens believe, are punished by the ancestors and by means of magic and witchcraft, but Christian Bantu believe that God is the ultimate sanction against sin. Bantu Christians readily submit to the authority of the Church (priests, elders and deacons) in matters appertaining to breaches of Christian faith and practice, both within the family and within the community. Although vestiges of pagan beliefs and practices are still found among Bantu Christians, personal and group behaviour are based on, generally speaking, Christian ethics and morality, and on the non-existence of hell, and of the promise of eternal life.

SELBY BANGANI NGCOBO

Mr. Ngcobo is an African. Born at Pietermaritzburg in 1908 of Christian parents, he was educated at Adams College and at the South African Native College, Fort Hare, where he took his Bachelor of Arts degree in 1931. In 1937 he took his Bachelor of Economics at the Natal University College, and then proceeded to Yale University, U.S.A. Here he graduated as a Master of Arts in 1940.

On his return to South Africa he taught at Adams High School and was appointed principal of Loram Secondary School, Durban, in 1944. He is now Research Fellow in African Economics at the University of Natal.

CHAPTER VI

The Coloured Community

GEORGE J. GOLDING and
FRANKLIN PYBUS JOSHUA

THERE are 1,000,000 people of mixed racial origin in South
Africa to whom the name ' Coloured ' is applied. Included in
these are a small section of what are known as Cape Malays,
who, whilst classified as Coloured persons, nevertheless differ
from the latter in respect of their religion and culture, which is
essentially Muslim and eastern in outlook.

Very few positive definitions of Coloured people have been
made by the various Government Commissions which have been
set up to investigate the problems of the Coloured population
thus far. Practically every definition of a Coloured man has been
in the form of a statement indicating what the Coloured people
are not, leaving the actual and positive definition as an open
question.

The Coloured people are the offspring of parents of three
main groups, the Europeans who landed at the Cape, the eastern
slaves imported into the Cape, and the aboriginal races (Bushmen, Hottentots and Africans) which inhabited various parts of
South Africa.

As a result of the inter-marriage there exists to-day a considerable group of Coloured persons who have invaded practically
every walk of life, and who are most numerous in the Cape
Peninsula and the Western Province of the Cape of Good Hope.
It is estimated that slightly more than 50 per cent of the
Coloured population is to be found in the Western Cape, with
a less concentrated yet appreciable group in the Eastern
Province, a small but significant group in the Transvaal, and a
lesser accumulation in the Orange Free State and Natal. For

purely descriptive purposes, we can divide the Coloured people into the following groups :

(1) Those who resemble the typical European in appearance and racial features.

(2) The group which approximates most nearly to the aboriginal stock, and

(3) The section which is midway in racial character between the two former types.

In the first group we have those persons who are regarded as semi-Whites, and who refer to themselves as being Coloured Europeans. There are reasons why such persons are referred to as being semi-Whites. To the visitor to Cape Town, whether he be an Imperial soldier or a tribal African from the Native Territories, such persons would in the ordinary way be regarded as a member of South Africa's European population. In outlook and appearance they resemble the average European, possessing fair skins, long straight hair, which may be black, brown or fair, sharp noses, thin lips and light eyes. Closely related to this group is the section which, except for being slightly darker in complexion, is of a similar strain. Due to the fortuitous shuffling of the colour-genes in the mechanism of inheritance, members of the same family are known to be alike in all respects but for their skin colour. The closeness with which this group resembles the average European in South Africa depends on the extent to which the characteristics of their European forbears have been dominant. There are, at the present time, very few Coloured families where the European father or mother is still alive. It is usually the second or third generation that is being carried on to-day, and by means of inter-marriage with groups of more or less similar racial make-up, a fairly significant percentage of European-like children result, whilst a number of darker-skinned offspring complete the family circles.

The chief racial elements that have contributed to this group are the English, Irish, Welsh, Scotch, French, South African Europeans on the one side, and Indian, Chinese and aboriginals on the other. Not only the so-called Cape Coloured persons, who constitute 75 per cent of the Coloureds, are found in the group, but also those sections of the Griquas and Namaqualanders which have been mixed with European blood.

The second group of Coloured people is light to dark brown in colour, and possesses a racial structure which can conveniently be described as being typically Coloured. These have straight, black hair, brown or black eyes, broad forehead, slightly flattened nose and fairly thin lips. As is to be expected a large amount of variation is present in this group; the complexion ranges from light-coloured to dark-skinned, hair texture varies from long and straight to short and wavy or frizzy and from light brown to black in colour, whereas the features show diversity in thinness of the lips, height of the bridge of the nose and the colour of the eyes.

One remarkable peculiarity of this group of Coloured people is the manner in which the various racial characteristics differ in members of the same family, between groups of families and between persons from various districts. A Coloured girl may have what is regarded as European features, and her hair may be frizzy or Bushmanlike; another may have long ginger-coloured hair, yet the cheek-bones may be high and prominent, the nose broad or flat. Some persons have vivid blue eyes with short stiff hair and flat features, and others, who may possess sharp delicate features, have brown eyes, dark skins and frizzy hair.

The third group of Coloured people are those who show racial affinity with the Africans, the Bushmen and the Hottentots. The great majority of them are very dark in colour and in general appearance will be indistinguishable from the type of person ordinarily taken to be a Native.

They have short woolly hair, usually black eyes, broad flat noses and thick lips. If the individual has relationship to the brown aboriginals the skin colour is not as dark brown as those with affinities with the African, and the hair, although hard, short and frizzy, is longer. It is becoming increasingly difficult to draw the line between this type of Coloured person and the true African or Bushman, because of the frequency of inter-marriage that is taking place in those areas where large communities of Coloured people and Natives live side by side under identical conditions. This is especially true of the larger centres in the North West Cape and certain spots in the Transkeian Native territories.

To these groups must be added the Mauritians, who, though

they do not consider themselves ' Coloured,' being offspring of the Mauritians of French Territory, are so classified for official purposes.

In such a diverse classification it is not surprising to find degrees of class and race distinctions which express colour attitudes, the near-Whites displaying similar prejudices as are seen among the Whites. Indeed many Coloured persons consider themselves superior to Indians, refusing the professional services of Indians as doctor and the like. This is more marked in territories where the Coloureds are few in numbers as in Natal.

The social status enjoyed by Coloured people depends upon the type of employment in which they are engaged, which in turn has a bearing on the amount of education which Coloured people are able to give their children.

The vast majority of Coloured persons are employed in the most poorly-paid jobs, such as unskilled farm labourers and domestic servants. Another large group is engaged as semi-skilled labourers and skilled operatives in factories. Coloured men have a recognized aptitude for performing work of a creative nature, and there is a large group of Coloured artisans, who are engaged as fully-qualified bricklayers, plasterers, carpenters, joiners, cabinet makers, printers, sheet-metal workers, mechanics, welders, duco-sprayers, upholsterers and french polishers. The wages received by Coloured persons in these occupations are those governed by wage agreements and industrial council determinations in the respective industries.

Coloured artisans have willingly fallen into line with the dictum that there should be no inequality between the wages paid to the respective racial groups, with the result that it is only the Coloured artisan who receives equal pay for equal work. In every other walk of life the Coloured worker receives unequal pay for equal work, and even the Coloured teacher to-day receives in the Cape Province only four-fifths of the salary paid to a European teacher with equal qualifications.

There has been a steady and significant decline in the number of Coloured youths apprenticed in the various trades each year. It should be mentioned that the Apprenticeship Act in South Africa contains no legal discrimination against the Coloured population. But the absence of legal bars to apprenticeship has not assisted in having Coloured youths accepted as suitable candidates by the various apprenticeship committees throughout the country. One reason is the general prejudice which exists against persons of colour being given opportunities to qualify for admittance to the relatively well-paid jobs as artisans. The employers of labour are almost exclusively Europeans, and it lies within their power to accept or reject applications from Coloured youths as apprentices. The tendency is for these employers to give preference to European youths, and it is with the greatest difficulty that a Coloured youth receives an opening to enter the motor, printing, engineering, building, furniture and electrical industries.

The Union Government itself has given a lead in this matter by safeguarding the interests of European labour. The South African Railways and Harbours Administration, which controls the state-owned railways, and which is one of the largest employers of labour in the country, has persistently confined its labour as far as possible to Whites.

As far as clerical and professional jobs are concerned, a few Coloured persons occupy positions as clerks in the Government service and in private businesses. Coloured youths find it well-nigh impossible to become articled in the legal profession, and for many years not a single Coloured man was able to qualify as a lawyer. Only recently did a Coloured teacher succeed in being admitted as an Attorney to the Cape Bar, and three or four students are undergoing training as articled clerks to firms of lawyers in Cape Town. The field of accountancy is practically closed to Coloured youths, as well as the profession of pharmacy. In both these, the professional Societies are unwilling to accept Coloured youths as articled clerks or registered apprentices. Coloured students are allowed to qualify for the medical profession in the universities of Cape Town and Witwatersrand, and there are in the Union to-day a fair number of fully qualified Coloured medical practitioners who have obtained their training in the Union. It is the Government's intention to concentrate non-European medical and dental education at the University of Natal.

Education is in the hands of the four Provincial Departments. The standard varies in accordance with the policy of the authority concerned. For instance that of the Cape Province is looked upon as more liberal and generous than that of the Orange Free State and the Transvaal, whereas Natal attempts to keep pace with that of the Cape. The greatest concentration of Coloured people occurs in the Western Cape Province, where educational facilities for the Coloureds are the best in the country, though still inadequate to meet the need. Education is compulsory by statute, but in practice there are many hundreds of Coloured children who do not receive it, and of those who are able to take advantage of the opportunities few continue their schooling beyond the primary standards. The intelligence quotient of the Coloured child is lower than that of the European child, a fact due in large measure to the social and economic environment. Many thousands are called upon to leave school in order to supplement the family income. Of every hundred pupils enrolled in 1935 in Standard I, only twenty-seven reached Standard VI in 1940. Only some 5 per cent who finish the primary-school period reach the matriculation standards. These figures illustrate the influence of economic incapacity as well as the absence of opportunity in education.

Politically the Coloured people lie somewhere between the Natives and the Europeans. At the beginning of the 19th century they were recognized as enfranchised people. As long ago as 1828 it was set down in Ordinance, ' That all Hottentots and other free persons of colour lawfully residing in the Colony are, and shall be, entitled to all the rights and privileges and benefits of the law to which any other of his Majesty's subjects are entitled.' After the abolition of slavery in 1834 and at the elections of the Municipality of Cape Town, Coloured persons enjoyed the vote on the same basis as White persons. In the Cape there were no changes in the political status, and there as in Natal they enjoyed the franchise, whereas in the Transvaal and the Orange Free State it was withheld from them. With the Act of Union a Colour Bar was introduced, but Coloured men were not excluded from being elected as members of the Provincial Council and Municipalities in the Cape Province and Natal. The proportion of Coloured voters in the Cape was influential at the elections until the franchise was extended to European women.

There were about 55,000 Coloured voters on the roll in the
Cape Province in 1946. The number of voters in 1953 had fallen
to 47,000.

The tendency now is that the Coloured people will be placed
on a separate roll and will elect one of their own number to a
Coloured representative council which in its turn will elect a
certain number of European members of Parliament. These
members will have limited power in Parliamentary divisions. It
is not intended, for example, that they shall vote on questions of
war and peace or on subjects dealing with the political status of
non-Europeans. In a word the Coloured people will come under
the legislative design to which the term *apartheid* has been
given, a plan to separate the races in residence and status.

The Coloured people are so diverse in origin, in economic
attainment and in individual characteristics that they cannot
easily be classified. To-day it is probably true that they are
gradually becoming a distinct race, and that a community sense
is growing among them. At the same time we cannot disregard
the fact that at the lower levels the Coloured man seeks his salvation nearer the Native and at the higher levels he endeavours
to be classed as a European. There are good reasons for both
these fringing movements. In the middle, however, the Coloured
people have no desire to be considered anything but a distinct
community. In the past they have enjoyed political rights with
the Europeans, and it is not surprising to find that they look
upon themselves as nearer the Europeans than as allied to the
Natives or Indians. Their great desire is to make their own
contribution to the nation of which they peculiarly are a part.
The Government proposes that a new department shall be established, with a Minister of Coloured Affairs at its head, to give
attention to the community. The Coloured people themselves
prefer to remain on the previous system which included their
name on the common voters' roll with Europeans and to take
their chances of development in that way rather than be segre-
gated under the new design.

There are one or two political parties to which reference
should be made. In 1902 the African Political Organization
was formed to advance the rights of Coloured people. It failed
to obtain the franchise for Coloured men in the Transvaal and

the Orange Free State, and again in 1930, when European women were enfranchised, it did not succeed in obtaining similar rights for Coloured women. All it could do in the circumstances was, and is, to give its support to the European political party showing the most sympathy with its interests. The Coloured vote has little effect on the policy of any party, and to-day the major fear is that the rights as set down in the entrenched clauses of the Constitution will be abolished.

Persuaded that some agency should be established for the airing of grievances the Government set up a Coloured Advisory Council consisting of twenty members appointed by the Government. The creation of this body caused a serious rift in the community, its opponents being convinced that the Coloured Advisory Council was merely a tool in the Government's hands for the permanent segregation of the Coloureds. As a result of this schism, and of the policy of the Government to erase Coloureds from the common roll, there has appeared, what did not before exist, a definite move to unite with other non-European groups for the furtherance of a common cause. The African People's Organization has been captured by the opponents of the Advisory Council and possesses a vigorous policy of non-European unity. There are, however, other elements who view this movement with grave disapproval and who, like the Coloured People's National Union, support the Coloured Advisory Council and insist that the salvation of the community lies not in political unity with Natives but as a distinct and separate community. The A.P.O., on the other hand, now rejects collaboration with the present Nationalist Government and accepts members other than Coloureds, moving inevitably towards the militant Indian groups organized under the Congress Party.

GEORGE J. GOLDING

Mr. George J. Golding, J.P., was born at Ladysmith, Cape, on May 28th, 1906. He qualified at Zonnebloem Training College as a teacher and became Principal of St. Barnabas C.E. School, Heidelberg, Cape, in 1922, and later at Bethel Institute, Cape Town. He is now head of Ashley Higher Primary School.

Mr. Golding was organizer and executive official to the first

National Convention of Coloured people in 1937 and served as chairman of the Coloured Advisory Council—a government-appointed body—from 1944 to 1949. He is now president of the Coloured People's National Union, which has a membership of 1800, and also the Chairman of the National Convention Co-ordinating Committee. In addition to serving on many Coloured organizations as executive member, he was editor of the *Teachers' League Journal* and the *Teachers' Educational and Professional Association* for several years. He holds the Bishop's licence as a lay reader in the Church of the Province of South Africa.

Mr. Golding is a Justice of the Peace—the first Coloured man to hold this office in the Union.

As a young man he was a prominent sportsman, winning the South African Coloured singles and doubles tennis championships.

FRANKLIN PYBUS JOSHUA

Franklin Pybus Joshua was born in Kimberley on December 21st, 1916. Educated at William Pescod High School, Kimberley, and the S.A. Native College, he graduated as a Bachelor of Science at the University of South Africa and took the diploma of Education in 1936.

After some teaching experience he proceeded to the University of Cape Town and conducted post-graduate research work of Coloured education. He was awarded the Bachelor of Education degree, after which he entered the Public Service in a specially graded post as secretary to the Coloured Advisory Council and acted in that capacity until January, 1950. He is now teaching at the South Peninsula Secondary School, Southfield, Cape Town.

He is an executive member of the Coloured People's National Union and honorary secretary to the National Association of Coloured Government Employees. He is interested in journalism, and is married and has four children.

CHAPTER VII

The Indian Community

G. H. CALPIN

THE arrival of Indians in South Africa originated in a demand
for cheap and reliable labour for the sugar plantations on the
east coast in Natal at a time, 1860, when the Zulus proved unwilling to work for long periods and were unaccustomed to the
needs of industry. Indian 'coolies' came under a scheme of
indentured employment formulated by the British Government
in co-operation with the Government of India and the local
authorities in Natal. Indian labourers contracted to serve three,
or later five years, at the end of which period they had the choice
of prolonging their contract, of returning to India or of accepting
a grant of land in lieu of a free passage to India.

The majority chose to become free labourers; a few chose to
re-indenture with their employers. The gap left in the labour
force was filled by the arrival of more 'coolies.' Their presence
as free labourers was valuable in providing labour for a variety
of industrial and domestic needs in the developing colony. So
long as Indians remained under contract as labourers no objec-
tions were raised. It was when they became free labourers that
protests were heard. Even then, however, the protests were less
against the 'emancipated coolie' than against those who, following in the wake of the labourers, came as traders and shopkeepers. Most of the labourers were Hindus; most of the traders
were Muslims, with a sprinkling of Gujerati Hindus, the Hindu
trading class.

As the numbers of both increased, by immigration and by
births, the opposition of Europeans increased, but for a variety
of reasons employers of labour welcomed the cheap labour of the
'coolies.' European shopkeepers objected strongly to the competition of the Indian traders, who, it was said, lived ' on the smell

of an oil rag.' Soon there were demands that the entry of free Indians should cease, the attitude of Europeans depending upon their economic interests.

The fate of Indians rested somewhere between these interests and the history of Natal is notable for the competition between employers, who desired more and more cheap labour, and the European trading community, who demanded a cessation of immigration in order to stop Indian competition in trade. We find, then, legislation to import more labourers accompanied by legislation to prevent the settlement of Indians in the country. In this tug-of-war it was the employers of labour who won most of the rounds, for immigration did not cease until just before the outbreak of war in 1914, and only then at the instigation of the Government of India.

In 1874 there were over 30,000 free Indians in Natal. By 1911 the total number of Indians, free and indentured, was over 133,000.

It should be said at once that the Government of India welcomed this disposal of some of its Indian population, and was always ready to consider suggestions for a continuance of the traffic. An anxiety to dispose of the surplus population in this way probably accounts for the weakness of the policy of the Government of India towards early legislative measures in Natal designed to restrict free Indians in trade, to abolish the parliamentary franchise to which Indians were entitled as British subjects, and to restrain the movement of Indians. The restriction of Indian trading was made possible by placing its control under licensing officers appointed by town councils, a practice which continues to-day to curb Indians' trading activities and which forms one of the disabilities about which Indians never cease to complain.

Despite these restrictions the demand for fresh supplies of labourers persisted. For twenty years after 1874 the Natal Government set aside £10,000 annually as a subsidy to the cost of introducing Indian labourers, and as late as 1902, after the Anglo-Boer war, there was a demand for an additional supply of 15,000, a number less than the number of contract labourers who had finished their term and were now free to offer their labour and services on the open market. On the other hand, so serious was the number of free Indians entering—'passenger' Indians, they were called—that in 1896 the arrival of a ship-load led to open demonstration at the port of Durban, during which, it is interesting to note, Mr. Gandhi, who was now at the beginning of his career as 'a passive resister,' was saved from European anger by the police.

It was out of this situation, a complex of many factors, among which must be recorded the demand for labour, the commercial competition of free Indians, the increasing numbers of Asiatics whose religions, habits and customs offended Euro-peans, that what is called the Indian problem arose; a problem which has found its way to the United Nations Assembly on several occasions. By 1936 there were 183,661 Indians in Natal, the Indian rate of growth being sustained by a birth-rate of 37 per 1,000 as against 20 per 1,000 of Europeans.

Elsewhere in South Africa the story is a little different. There were practically no Indians in the Transvaal before 1881. After that date they must have arrived in considerable numbers, for within two or three years memorials were presented to the Volksraad urging that the influx should be restricted. A petition by the burgesses of Pretoria stated that 'the population of Arabs (traders) and coolies is much increased in this town and State,' spoke of their 'loathsome mode of living' and called for their 'isolation in their own locations.' As a result of this the famous Law 3 of 1885 was enacted which forbade Indians from acquir-ing citizenship rights in the Transvaal Republic and from own-ing landed property. Similar laws were passed after the Anglo-Boer war when the Transvaal became a Crown Colony. It was against them and the restrictions existing in Natal that Mr. Gandhi protested and gathered his followers in a passive resist-ance campaign.

Fearful of a repetition of the experience of the Transvaal, the Orange Free State forbade entry to Indians, so that in that terri-tory the number of Indians to-day amounts to no more than twenty.

In the Cape, however, whereas the number of Indians was originally small and even now is no more than 9,000, the restric-tions upon entry were not serious. At the time of Union of the four territories into the Union of South Africa, Indians were forbidden to move from province to province, a restriction which, with the initial settlement, explains their local concentrations throughout the country. Durban, for example, contains the largest Indian population of any city outside India, Indian numbers being almost equal to European. In 1940 the number of Indians in Natal had increased to 195,000, the figure for Europeans in the same year being 201,900.

The Indian population is extremely youthful. In 1936, 47 per cent of Indians were under 15 years of age and only 13 per cent over 45 years of age, by contrast with the European figures of 27 and 26 respectively. Professor H. R. Burrows, to whom we are indebted for much research on this question, estimates that by 1960 there will be at least 263,000 Indians in Natal. His comment is : ' On the lines of present tendencies it looks as though Natal should plan to build more houses and schools for the youthful Indian population and more hospitals and houses for the ageing European section.'

All told there are about 365,000 Indians in the whole country, and the question of their treatment and status forms one of the larger issues facing Europeans. Referring to the problem in the House of Assembly, General Smuts remarked that ' we are the victims of an historic mistake.' The mistake was that we did not arrange at the outset for the repatriation of Indian labourers, as we did for the Chinese who were imported to work on the goldfields. As a result central, provincial and local governments are beset by a multitude of anxieties, some of them localized but all of them touching our relations with India, and, through India, with the Commonwealth and the United Nations.

Various attempts have been made to grapple with these problems. The overall policy has been to get rid of as many Indians as possible by voluntary schemes of repatriation with financial compensation, and to restrict the movement and activities of those remaining. Whereas these schemes have succeeded in an outflow of some thousands and in segregating the remainder in allocated areas, no scheme has yet succeeded either in placating Indians or in appreciably affecting the population. Rather the reverse. The failure to ' solve ' the problem has irritated it. It has increased the fear that the problem is incapable of solution, and as a result has intensified the hostility between the races, particularly in congested areas like Durban.

The Indian problem is part of South Africa's colour problem. It must be set against the Native problem. Were there not eight million Natives, the presence of 365,000 Indians would not be the ' menace ' it is described. Were the Europeans not a small white majority on a large black continent, their fears would be less intense than they are. And, in addition, were there not many thousands of Indians in British East Africa, Kenya for example, strategic considerations about the supremacy of the White man would not impress South Africa with their significance.

Europeans in South Africa would prefer to engage with the United Nations in a large-scale transfer of Indian population to India, such as was effectively done with the Greeks from Turkey after the 1914-18 war. Locally, and on the assumption, a justifiable one, that the hope is remote for a large-scale transfer, the policy that appeals to Europeans, British and Afrikaners alike, is to segregate Indians in their own residential or group areas; to control their activities, especially their trading activities, within limits to sustain European supremacy; and to restrict their political representation. At the moment, Indians have no representation, direct or indirect, in Parliament and local governments, the attempts to give them representation by Europeans in Parliament having failed as a result of Indian refusal to participate in such indirect methods and also as a result of a change in government.

Indians in South Africa are separated into two main groups, Hindu and Muslim. In Natal in 1936 Hindus formed 81 per cent, Muslims less than 14 per cent, Christians 4 per cent, and others 1 per cent. At no time has South Africa had a cross section of India in its midst. Indians came here either as industrial labourers, with all that the term conveys in illiteracy, habits and customs, or as traders. Among Hindus the caste system disappears very slowly. The Hindu family is essentially matriarchal. Divorce is not allowed. The Muslim family is strictly patriarchal. The number of sub-divisions in each group makes a study of them impossible in a short essay. What is particularly to be noted among them is the joint-family system, especially marked among Hindus, a feature of which is the congregation under one roof of grandparents, parents, married sons and their children. This system, which often results in overcrowding and its accompanying deficiencies, is a safeguard in times of unemployment and depression. Early marriage, however, and the religious ban on birth control, test even the wisdom of this system, and to-day, as a result of various factors, it is gradually giving place to the adoption of the western custom of separate households.

A noticeable difference between Hindus and Muslims is the rate at which Hindu girls are taking advantage of what opportunities exist for education and economic advancement. Especially is this to be seen in the Tamil group. By contrast, the Muslim father is still reluctant to allow his daughters to go out into the world, and it is revealing to discover in a Muslim family of girls that only the youngest received the advantages of education, a fact which illustrates a gradual parental recognition of economic necessity.

At first sight Muslims appear richer than Hindus. Individually this is not always so. A feature of Muslim society is that Muslims spend more than Hindus. They are more ostentatious with their wealth, the successful merchants possessing American cars and fine houses. It is true, however, that the Hindus form the Indian labour force in the factories, on the farms, on the sugar plantations, and as clerks, waiters and the like. The opportunities for professional advancement are not extensive. Trading is the chief ambition of the many Hindus, even as it is the main occupation of Muslims. There are all manner of conventions and difficulties in the way of Indians who wish to become chartered accountants, chemists, engineers and the like. Industry forms little part of the ambitions of the well-to-do Indian. He is traditionally a trader. If he is a Muslim, his sons follow him in his business; a fact which makes most commercial houses family concerns, to the disadvantage of employee clerks, who are so often Hindus. The legal profession offers one outlet for the able youth, so do medicine and teaching, though the last-named, if secure, is not well paid.

Though it would be incorrect to suggest that the South African Indian community is an India in miniature, the communal differences which have marked India's history are to be seen here in less obvious, though not unimportant, ways.

Religious barriers exist to keep the two sections apart socially. Muslims and Hindus of the upper strata do not mix. A famous case in 1936, when the Agent-General for India in South Africa, a Muslim, married a local Hindu lady, led to serious domestic trouble and political rift among Indians. Even within each section, marriage is confined to family frontiers in the case of Muslims and to caste in the case of Hindus. In other activities, such as education, a line of division is to be seen operating to keep the sections apart.

The majority of Indians are South African born. Though they look to India as their motherland they are essentially colonials who would find life in India alien to their ways. They are becoming westernized in dress and speech. One of their problems is to retain their vernaculars. A Muslim, whose language is Gujerati, finds it difficult to follow the Gujerati of Karachi's news-broadcasts. All Indian children learn the vernacular at school, and this, with the religious education required, particularly in the case of Muslims who are called upon to memorize a part of the Q'uran, accounts for the fact that they are two or three years older than European children in matriculating.

This, of course, applies to those who are fortunate enough to obtain schooling. Many thousands of children do not go to school at all; there are not sufficient schools available, despite the increasing attention given to Indian education during the past few years. The adult generation is woefully lacking in education.

An important development of recent years is the appearance of the class struggle among them. In time this is likely to break down the communal divisions, though the 'labour versus capital' conflict, the poor versus the rich, takes on features already imposed by religion. On the whole Hindus and Muslims separate into Congress and Organization Parties. The Congress Party is representative of workers in the mass and the Indian Organization, moderate and conservative, is representative of the trading class. Indians, as Indians, have one aim : it is to become full citizens of South Africa, equal with Europeans. But Indians as workers and Indians as merchants have their respective aims which often conflict. Indians as workers seek to unite with workers of other races in the class struggle. The class struggle and the race struggle are now overlapping. There is a movement initiated by Indian leaders, a few of them avowed Communists, towards a non-European Front, united action by Natives, Indians and Coloureds for the advancement of a common cause. How far this movement has touched the mass of Natives is difficult to say, particularly since the Government has taken legislative steps to ban Communism. What is to be noticed is that the various restrictions imposed upon Indians are breaking down some of the religious barriers and encouraging unity in political action.

Indians in the mass are a law-abiding people and the appearance among them of militant political groups is new to South Africa. Between them and the Natives amicable relations have existed for many years. Latterly, however, some inter-racial clashes in Natal, and especially the riots at the beginning of 1949 in which over a hundred people were killed and great material damage done to property, have caused grave concern. Natives look upon Indians as intruders, not conquerors, and though Indian traders perform many services for Natives there is much resentment as a result of their presence. Natives are now demanding opportunities in trade and services. They are no longer content to be the servants and labourers, either of the European or the Indian. Many of them cannot understand why the Government has allowed Indians to buy land, open shops and build houses in the towns. Whereas in politics Indian leaders and Native leaders are beginning to co-operate, at other levels hostility exists which, it is reasonable to assume, thrives on the known hostile attitude Europeans show towards Indians.

Race attitudes are notoriously difficult to assess. Towards Europeans, Indians bring a feeling of bitterness as a result of their disabilities and frustrations. They do not, as a rule, distinguish between British and Afrikaners. They complain that the British in South Africa are as anti-Indian as Afrikaners. The most cordial commercial relations exist between Indians and Europeans as individuals and as trading concerns, and individually a degree of friendship is to be seen, and even respect and regard, though this does not reach to the interchange of social occasions. There are the usual differences between the official attitudes, which seek to restrict and curb Indian economic

PLATE VIII

AN INDIAN ARCADE IN DURBAN.

[*To face page* 86.

PLATE IX

advance, and non-official attitudes which accept Indians as part of the economic order. The same European who transacts business with an Indian, to the benefit of both, will in his turn refer to the Indian as a threat to European economy. At other levels the general attitude of Europeans is to accept the presence of Indians so long as their status is that of a servant. At bottom, race attitudes rest on fears of competition, economic, social and political, with the over-riding anxiety caused by the increasing numbers of Indians.

Such fears do not exist between Indians and Natives. The competition of Natives for employment and in trade is not serious enough to arouse anxiety and hostility. Indians are better equipped mentally for the economic struggle, and are no more conscious of Native competition than are Europeans. There is, however, one department in which Indians entertain anxiety. In unskilled and semi-skilled work Natives are often preferred to Indians, not necessarily because of skill but because of their docility and because of the increasing rift between Europeans and Indians. Europeans frown upon the political activities of Indians leading to ' hartals ' (strikes in which Indians are called to observe a day of prayer). Trade unionism is still in its infancy, and it is with great difficulty that Europeans and Indians unite in a trade union to give official impress to political protests regarding the treatment of Indians. They exist in the catering and liquor trade, where Indians are employed in great numbers as stewards and waiters, and in the furniture industry. The more usual practice is parallel trade unions, in which each race has a separate union in the same industry. On the whole it can be said that European workers do not welcome mixed trade unions, though there are considerable numbers of Indians in the Garment Workers, Textile Workers, and Leather Workers Union.

' Equal pay for equal work,' one of the slogans of Indian workers, has the effect of keeping Indians out of employment in difficult times, the choice of industrial employers (who are almost exclusively European) falling upon members of their own race. In the same way Government departments employ Europeans wherever possible and in the low-paid occupations Indians must compete with Natives.

Though there are many evidences of wealth among Indians, the community on the whole is poor, though not so poor as their fellows in India. Indeed all Indians realize that despite the disabilities imposed upon them they are better off in South Africa than they would be in India. It is a fear with many that they might be expatriated to India, though it is true that many thousands who were born in India have chosen to return.

As with all communities which do not enjoy the prerogatives of their rulers, Indians display remarkable tenacity and determination. In the ordinary way South Africa offers sufficient employment to them. What Indians lack is opportunity and openings in professional activities. The lack drives many into trade, shopkeeping and commission agencies, activities which are overcrowded. The effect is beneficial in one respect. Competition keeps prices down.

This is one of their contributions to the general economy. Like the Jews of early days, Indians were found penetrating the inland districts, serving European farms and Native settlements. Beyond their labour and their trading, each valuable in the competitive sense, the community has not been able to contribute to the general welfare. No poets, no artists, no philosophers came with the individual labourers and the traders. None has arrived since to give South Africa a true picture of India's culture. Occasionally, as in the case of Sir Srinivasa Sastri, the first Agent-General appointed to South Africa, a man appears representative of India who brings to Europeans the voice and culture of the East. It is then that Indians themselves appreciate how much they lack, and that Europeans gain a new appreciation of the Indian nation. Preoccupation of the Indian worker with his daily task, and a close attention to business by the trader, added to the political struggle for equality, allows no time and dulls the desire for those arts and sciences by which India is known in the world.

Asked what great gift Indians in South Africa have made to the common good, they might answer ' Mahatma Gandhi ', for it was in South Africa that Mr. M. K. Gandhi, as he was then, practised as a lawyer and later gave himself to the cause of humanity. But in addition, Indians would refer to the part they have played in the development of the sugar and other industries.

Absence of opportunity, lack of education, a sense of frustration which seems to drown what community sense is available, are the main reasons for the absence of great social or industrial achievement outside the field of trade. Malnutrition and poverty, the incidence of disease, particularly of tuberculosis, add their quota to the backwardness of many thousands.

Education and public health measures are increasingly encouraging. In the former there is a degree of self-help and an acknowledged scheme of state-aided schools, schools established by various Indian trusts, Muslim and Hindu, with the aid of grants from Provincial Governments. Schooling is being made progressively free, though in higher education opportunities are inadequate to meet the demand. There are, too, several excellent organizations of interested Europeans and Indians co-operating in welfare work. One that stands out as an example is the Friends of the Sick Association, an organization initiated by Europeans and now extended in settlements for the control of tuberculosis. In such work Europeans and Indians co-operate with great benefit. Then there is the rather special case of the Ismaili Muslims, numbering some thirty or forty families, living in Pretoria. These Muslims are followers of the Aga Khan and are under his oversight as their Imam. They enjoy the direction of the Aga Khan's special African Council, and in this way are privileged, as a result of their own endeavours and the help received, in possessing a variety of welfare schemes such as nursery schools.

One or two newspapers, one printed in English, others partly in English and partly in the vernacular, and published weekly, serve the community. Most of them are political and religious organs, the aim being to forward the aspirations of Indians at large. Indians are all agreed about their political aims. They claim they are South Africans, Indian South Africans. They have therefore no desire to live elsewhere. When they turn to India for aid in their struggle, it is for aid to become South Africans rather than to be looked on as Indians.

G. H. CALPIN

George Harold Calpin was born in 1897 in England and educated at the Friends School, Great Ayton, Yorkshire, and at Queens' College, Cambridge. He is a Master of Arts, and holds the Inter. B.Sc. (Econ.) degree. He was lecturer to the Board of Extramural Studies and the W.E.A., and science master and house tutor at Durham School, England.

In South Africa he became headmaster at Uplands School, Blackridge, Pietermaritzburg, and later was appointed Editor of *The Natal Witness,* a position he held for a number of years.

Mr. Calpin is the author of two books: *There are No South Africans* (1941) and *Indians in South Africa* (1949).

CHAPTER VIII

Education in South Africa

DR. O. D. WOLLHEIM

THE story of education during the past 300 years in what is now known as the Union of South Africa, is that of the efforts of a small outpost of western culture, cut off from the sources and mainsprings of their culture, and deposited in the midst of an overwhelming majority of peoples of a completely different culture, to maintain and strengthen their own way of life.

In very early days, shortly after the landing of van Riebeek in 1652, this struggle was not very difficult because the settlement was a closely-knit and well-organized one, but the pioneering spirit and intransigent independence of the early settlers soon dispersed the community into a straggling and widely scattered string of large farms which could only maintain some form of very occasional communication at long intervals. The advent of the British at the close of the 18th century and the subsequent Great Trek served to disperse the population still further, and to complicate matters by the introduction of a new language and a foreign political and cultural pattern. By the end of the 19th century the heirs to western culture still numbered fewer than the population of a sizeable European city, and were scattered from Cape Town to Pietersburg, and from Port Nolloth to St. Lucia Bay. They found themselves in the midst of a number of indigenous cultures practised by people who outnumbered them by eight to one, and whose strength lay in the fact that they were still living in closely-knit and well-organized tribal groups. Those far from the Cape found themselves more than ever cut off because of the enormous distances and slow communications.

A bare fifty years ago, then, there were still no integrated forms of education beyond the more closely settled areas of the Cape Colony, and outside of a few of the larger inland towns and mission stations. The inevitable result was widespread illiteracy among non-Europeans (who had for the most part never made any real acquaintance with western standards) and very low standards of literacy among large sections of the European people, who were big landowners and who governed the country.

The frequent upheavals in the history of South Africa have complicated matters further by the creation of powerful and quite natural antagonisms. The original founders of the country found that control over their country had been wrested from them and that they were being forced into patterns they did not like or understand. The inevitable frontier difficulties exasperated them. Soon after leaving to found a new life consonant with their own patterns, the discovery of diamonds and gold flooded them once again with very large groups of foreigners from all corners of the globe. The new elements which migrated into the country could not understand the mentality and did not appreciate the independence of the pioneer who had had little or no education, and who certainly had never had any real contacts with the sources of his culture for over 100 years. The Anglo-Boer War, which was the result of all these factors and others, exacerbated the antagonisms and strengthened the internal patriotisms within the colonies which emerged. Only as late as 1908 could the first steps towards union be contemplated, and even then the representatives who forged the union met in uneasy friendship and were only able to accomplish their task by accepting large-scale compromises which to some extent undermined the very unity they were seeking.

Other antagonisms, no less important and powerful, have also grown between the governing and the governed. The efforts of the early missionaries led to the establishment of large numbers of schools for the non-European groups, but these missions had not the resources to cater for the millions requiring their work. As a result there has been the growth of a small non-European aristocracy of educated, literate and cultured persons bitterly opposed to the policies of the European, who fears that full status will lead to swamping, and is determined to maintain his racial and cultural identity. The tremendous but yet incoherent struggle for freedom of the illiterate and semi-illiterate masses of

Africans is being canalized through this aristocracy into an up-surge of non-European nationalisms.

It is against this backcloth of stresses and strains that the picture of education in South Africa should be viewed. Without it the various streams and movements become inexplicable, the system and method of administration irrational and the general direction obscure.

The story began shortly after the first European settlers landed in 1652, with the appointment of a ' Ziekentrooster ' (comforter of the sick) whose business it was to visit the sick and to teach the children. All races attended and the son of an important official of the Dutch East India Company shared a desk with the daughter of a Malay slave, or a child of one of the Hottentot servants. At a later stage individual farmers or groups of farmers appointed private tutors who were for the most part broken-down officials, deserters or renegades, and who were appointed solely because they had soft white hands indicating that they did not do manual work and because they could read and write. Outside the larger towns and mission stations this system of private tutoring remained in vogue throughout the country until close upon the turn of the last century. These ' Meesters ' were an important part of the social system because they wrote many of the letters, taught the children, acted as law agents for draw-ing deeds of sale and contracts, and generally acted as advisers in any matters involving the power to read and write.

The early basis of all teaching was religion, and the Bible was the source of all knowledge and information. The only reason for learning to read and write was to be able to consult the Bible when in doubt. All knowledge of geography, history and the sciences was gained from the same medium, and the lessons in the schools were largely confined to the learning of long passages to be recited from the Bible, and the singing of the psalms and hymns.

The real development of education did not commence until almost two centuries after the first settlers arrived. In 1839 Mr. James Rose Innes was appointed the first Superintendent-General of Education in the Cape Colony, and at about the same time the first missionaries started their work among non-European people. During the next fifty years there was considerable development in the Cape Colony, which took the form of grants-in-aid by the State to schools on a proportional basis to the amounts locally collected, the broadening of the syllabus, the institution of a system of inspection. The missionaries also established small stations which were later to become very large and famous institutions. Gradually in the state-aided, and later in the Government schools, the tendency was more and more to accept only European children, but in the mission schools children of all races continued to be educated side by side until after the end of the 19th century.

The first beginnings of a system were also to be found in the colony of Natal, and in the independent republic of the Orange Free State at about the same time. In Natal, Dr. Mann was appointed Director of Education in 1859; in the Orange Free State the Governor of the Cape Colony, Sir George Grey, made a donation of £5,000 for the establishment of what has become the Grey College and the University College of the Orange Free State. In the Transvaal the system remained very small, and as late as 1870 the whole vote for the education of the children of some 35,000 inhabitants was £1,575, most of which was spent on the salaries of sixteen permanent, and some itinerant, teachers. Fairly large-scale developments took place in the mission field during this period. Some fifty missionaries arrived about 1820, and the first government grants were made in 1841 and revised on an improved scale in 1865, when the system of inspection by government officials was tightened up.

During these years the content of the educational system remained narrow, and only with the greatest difficulty was it possible to introduce secular studies of the sciences and humanities. Strangely enough, this did not apply to the missions, which in early days introduced forms of industrial education by manual training, gardening, printing and bookbinding, etc.

The real development of education on modern lines only commenced with the appointment of Sir Thomas Muir in the Cape towards the close of the 19th century. He raised the minimum educational standards for recruits to the teaching profession, and founded a number of teacher-training colleges; a system of 'good service allowances' was instituted whereby good and faithful teachers earned bonuses; a redeemable loan system enabled local authorities to erect and equip undenominational schools; an educational library was started at headquarters; school boards were created, with paid officials to administer locally the educational system; the curriculum was modernized and liberalized by the inclusion of singing, needlework, woodwork, drawing, nature study and cookery; important educational surveys were made; secondary schools were strengthened, and a number of high schools created in order to prepare pupils for the university colleges, which now concentrated on postmatriculation studies only. Between 1909 and 1911 he introduced compulsory education for European children. Muir laid the foundations of the present system of education, and most of his reforms were later copied by the other parts of the country. He was a far-sighted, able and enthusiastic educationist and administrator, and his influence penetrated throughout the whole machine. He remained at the head of affairs until 1915, when he retired.

During the last decade of the 19th century significant developments also took place elsewhere in South Africa. In the Orange Free State a system of compulsory education for Europeans up to the age of 16 was introduced in 1897 (actually before the Cape Colony) by the Rev. John Brebner, another able and far-sighted educationist. He, too, instituted teacher-training, and took over the itinerant teacher system. The Transvaal system was immensely complicated by the growing tensions between Boer and Uitlander, after the discovery of gold. The Director of Education was Dr. Mansvelt, a determined and competent person. He tightened up the system of inspection, closed down inefficient schools, instituted a very liberal method of finance, and created high and training schools. During this time there was a continuous struggle between the Government which insisted on Dutch as the only medium of instruction, and the Council of Education, a voluntary organization representing the ' Uitlanders ', who refused to agree. This struggle continued after the Boer War, until the granting of responsible government to the Transvaal in 1906. During this period the policy of the Government, with Lord Milner at its head, was deliberately to denationalize and ' anglicize ' the Boers. As a result, there was the growth of a large number of Dutch private opposition schools known as the Christelik Nationaal Onderwijs Scholen, under the aegis of the Dutch Reformed Church. These schools were nationalized when General J. C. Smuts became Minister of Education under the Transvaal Responsible Government, by the simple but statesmanlike expedient of mother-tongue instruction.

A similar policy was adopted in the Orange Free State in 1908 by General Hertzog. In Natal there were no significant developments until the granting of Responsible Government in 1893, when an Education Department was constituted and proper authority vested in the Director. The growth from then onwards was similar to that of the other areas, except that the Natal Department has always retained more centralized power than any other.

The education of the non-Europeans appears to have been the almost exclusive prerogative of the Cape Colony, and to some extent Natal, where by the end of the century large establishments such as Lovedale, Zoonebloem, Tigerkloof, Adams College and a very large number of smaller schools had been established by the missionaries and assisted by the Governments.

This very short review of the main educational developments covers a period of 250 years, and can only indicate briefly the most important features. The period was one of immense difficulty, in which proud and independent spirits had to make painful adjustments to new situations, in which a new life had to be carved out of an untouched and unknown country, and which had enjoyed more than its share of bloody wars, invasions, rebellions, and riots. That the four independent states were so soon after the Boer war ready to meet and thrash out the basis for Union says much for the good sense and far-sightedness of all sections of the communities, except always, of course, the irreconcilables. The Act of Union was ratified in 1910, under very great difficulties. The Cape, which had traditionally followed a liberal policy towards non-Europeans and had given them the franchise and as many schools as they could, refused to give way to pressure from the North to abolish this franchise; rival claims for the location of the capital were made; it was difficult to know how to integrate the existing four parliaments into the new system; the four educational systems were jealously regarded by each; the unfortunate experiences of the North with

Milner and Dr. Jameson, the fears of small and weak Natal gave rise to intense suspicions. Inevitably wide compromises had to be made in order to achieve unity. In the educational field it was decided to give control over the ordinary primary and secondary schools to the newly-constituted Provincial Councils, successors to the former Parliaments, and control over 'higher' education to the new Union Parliament.

The Union of South Africa has therefore five Education Departments, one for each Province to control the ordinary schools of each, and one central Department which supervises universities, and has, since the Union, developed a wide system of technical schools, schools for the physically and mentally retarded, industrial and vocational schools, and a number of other miscellaneous educational institutions, all of which it wholly controls.

Except for the provincial schools in Natal, where control is largely centralized in the Education Department, the generally-accepted system of control in all institutions is for the relevant Department to control policy and for a large measure of autonomy to be left in the hands of local committees acting under statutory School Boards. In the Provincial schools, the Department owns the building and the grounds and provides free of charge certain minimum essential equipment and requisites. Anything above the minimum (which varies from Province to Province) must be obtained by local effort subsidized by the Department. A similar system, but much more liberally financed, obtains for the institutions controlled by the Union Education Department. The financing of the technical colleges is a subsidy based, under formula, upon the amount raised locally in fees and donations. There has thus been a struggle developing between these schools and the Provincial schools for pupils. The technical colleges have instituted courses which are actually the prerogative of the ordinary school, and, since they are able to offer much more attractive conditions, there has been a gradual landslide in the larger towns at about the age of puberty from the normal schools to the technical colleges.

In the case of non-Europeans, most schools are owned by the various missions of the various churches and societies although the State is tending more and more to accept responsibility through normal channels and is erecting school-board schools under committees. In the mission schools the Department pays the salaries of the teachers, provides certain requisites free, pays a rent grant based on the capital cost of the building and inspects the school. The school is administered by a Manager, who is usually the Missionary or Minister of the area, and who is a law unto himself. Non-Europeans tend more and more to resent this type of administration and to agitate for a completely state-controlled system.

The system is far from ideal and has resulted in many anomalies and much overlapping. From time to time teachers and educational reformers have started campaigns to end the system, but the vested interest in education held by the Provinces is too strong. Although the content of the syllabuses, and the standards are similar, there are yet significant differences which cause hardship on persons moving from Province to Province. Up to quite recently there were five different salary scales for teachers and there has always been friction between the various Departments when changes are mooted. What uniformity has been achieved has been voluntary through a consultative committee representative of the various Provinces.

In spite of these handicaps very great progress has been made since the Union. Perhaps the most important advance made during the past 100 years is the transformation of the teaching force from a number of vagabond itinerant teachers and parasitical ne'er-do-wells into an efficient and highly qualified force of able and devoted men and women. Teachers in the secondary area have almost without exception a university degree and at least one year of professional training. In the primary area these standards are also becoming more general, although a two-year post-matriculation course is the minimum demanded. In schools for non-Europeans most of the teachers are non-European, and although many of these teachers have the same qualifications as their white colleagues, the time has not yet arrived when the supply of matriculated scholars is sufficient to demand this as a minimum entrance examination for the profession.

After many years of struggle the teachers have gained for themselves a salary much nearer the cost of living than they have ever yet achieved. Living is very expensive in South Africa, and although the figures quoted below may appear high to some, they actually represent a standard of living which only just reaches respectability. The head of a high school of over 300 pupils, in possession of a degree and professional certificate, has a salary starting at £980 per annum and increasing by £40 per annum to £1,100. A similarly qualified head of a primary school of medium size would start at £800, and proceed by £30 increments to £950. Assistant teachers are paid £400 + £25 up to £800 in the secondary school and £350+£25 up to £700 in the primary school. These are salaries for males, those for females being four-fifths of them.[1] Salaries for Coloured (of mixed descent) persons are four-fifths those of Europeans while those for Africans average about one half of the European salaries. On the whole the general body of teachers is good but unimaginative. Industry, commerce, and the other professions, offer remuneration many times greater, so that the brighter pupils tend to avoid the choice of teaching as a future career. The approach of most teachers is one of deep interest in their pupils and a genuine desire to help and guide them. Much time is spent on sports fields, camps, excursions, and other extramural activities, although the stranglehold of external examinations tends to stifle originality and personality.

The examination bogey is in South Africa a very real one. In 1858, a Board of Examiners was set up to examine candidates for Matriculation. In almost one hundred years which have elapsed since its institution there have been few changes, and basically the examination is the same. The universities have consistently refused or been prevented from instituting their own entrance examinations, preferring the cheaper course of accepting the set external examination. The Provincial Education Departments have maintained a long and consistent struggle to humanize the secondary course, but have failed to move the Matriculation Board very much. The strength of the latter has been the general ignorance of industrial and commercial interests who use the certificate as a badge of economic value in fixing wages. As a result the secondary course has tended to be straitjacketed into the requirements of this examination, and the primary schools perforce prepare their pupils for the secondary course.

[1] European teachers received small salary increases in 1952.

On the whole the primary school is free to choose its course in consultation with a departmental inspector, as long as it satisfies the requirements of the final primary examination in a few subjects. More and more schools are experimenting with activity methods, age-grouping, intelligence and aptitude testing, and assignment methods, but in the main the primary school follows the traditional syllabus fairly methodically. The secondary schools all teach the two official languages, one science from a number of options, one philosophy from similar options, and two other subjects from a long list of practical and academic syllabuses. The secondary school-leaving examination demands a score of 30 per cent in each of at least five subjects, and a minimum of 40 per cent in the aggregate. A pass in the home language is essential; the requirements of the university entrance matriculation are a little stricter. Under such conditions it would be natural to expect a very wide range of intelligences and aptitudes to pass this examination, although South African students compare very well with similarly qualified students in Britain. The danger is that done to the personality of the high-spirited youths with specialized aptitudes when they are forced to accommodate themselves to the four-year secondary straitjacket.

It is interesting to analyse the actual attendances at school of the various racial groups in South Africa. The latest available figures (approximated) for the whole Union are as follows :—

(1950)	Attendances	Population	Percentage of Pop.
EUROPEAN	505,000	2,600,000	19·4
COLOURED AND ASIATIC ...	269,000	1,420,000	18·9
AFRICAN	774,000	8,400,000	9·2

The high percentage of attendances among Europeans is due to compulsory education from the age of six to various upper limits, and to the liberal financial aid to technical and other central government institutions catering mainly for Europeans. In the Cape Province a permissive ordinance sanctions the introduction of compulsion for Coloured pupils where there are sufficient schools, but this has only been applied in one small town. It says much for the various non-European groups of South Africa that, in spite of their extreme poverty and generally low standard of literacy, they have attained such high percentages of attendance. In the same year there were 45,305 teachers teaching just over 1,500,000 pupils in the provincial schools, making an average of just over 30 pupils per teacher. The total State expenditure on education of all races in the provincial schools in 1949 was £27,600,000, of which £18,608,000 was spent on some 500,000 European pupils, and the rest on over 900,000 non-European pupils. This works out at just over £50 per European pupil, and almost £10 per non-European.

Rather more than half of the European pupils pass at the age of about 14 into secondary schools, and about half of these again reach the school-leaving (matriculation) stage at the age of 18. Some 5 per cent of European scholars eventually reach the Universities. Among African children about 45 per cent of those of school-going age attend school, and of these more than half are in the kindergarten, and first primary grade. Some 5 per cent of these starting actually finish the primary course and an infinitesimal percentage ever reach the matriculation stage.

There are five universities of very high standard, of which four are old-established, one university college which in 1949 obtained its charter, and three constituent colleges of the University of South Africa (largely an examining body).

There is also a University college for Africans at Fort Hare. A full range of teaching faculties is offered by these Universities, the largest of which are at Cape Town and Johannesburg; the latter two admit non-Europeans who can afford it to their classes freely; to some extent research has been stifled by lack of adequate funds and by the use of formal classroom methods tending to kill the inquiring spirit.

Much is occurring in the educational field in South Africa at present. The last war necessitated the training of large numbers of skilled men by using methods which short-circuited the outdated apprenticeship system; the overlapping between provincial and central government schools caused more and more difficulty. A Government Commission was set up and reported in 1948 on the position (U.G.65/1948). Far-reaching changes are suggested in this report, many of which are in line with the suggestions of the Hadow and Spens reports. The main suggestions are the setting up of a Junior High School to take early adolescents and to give them guidance in personal problems and direction in the future, the revision and modernization of technical and vocational training, and the circumvention of the evils of divided control.

The value of parent/teacher co-operation is being realized more and more and there has been a rapid growth of Parent/Teacher Associations doing very good work. The spirit of teaching is becoming more and more liberal, and there is a greater sense of unity between teacher and taught. There is ever-growing irritation at the limitations of the secondary curriculum which tends to transform that branch of education into mere feats of memory and to kill the critical and inquiring spirit. The teachers show more solidarity than ever before and are at present agitating for a charter which would give them greater professional status, certain powers of discipline over themselves, and a say in the training, certification, and admission of candidates to the profession, but there is still no agreement among European teachers as to whether non-Europeans should be admitted to the terms of the charter.

There has been great interest in recent years in physical education and in adult education. Under the aegis of the Union Department of Education, two national boards to tackle these problems have been established with annual grants of money from Parliament which they are empowered to spend at their discretion. Physical education has shown great strides in the few years of its existence, and the Division of Adult Education is in the formative and exploratory stage. Each of these Boards will subsidize local efforts in their respective fields, but these fields have not yet been clearly defined and there is friction among these two divisions, and the Department of Social Welfare. There are very many social, cultural, and sporting voluntary associations, which also operate in these fields both among Europeans and non-Europeans. Probably the greatest part of the widening horizons of the lower income groups are due to the activities of such associations. Perhaps the greatest force of all is the cinema. Few South Africans, outside of the illiterate tribal groups, allow a week to pass without attending a cinema at least once. The influence of the cinema is hard to assess accurately, but, judging by the hold it has over the population, it must be powerful. The cinemas in South Africa are, however, almost all controlled by a powerful monopoly which tends to import mainly the cheaper and more sensational Hollywood type of film.

South Africa is in the melting pot. A small part of its European population has been educated for generations. The remainder is now in the first and second generation of education. Her non-European groups are in all stages of emergence from tribalism; the Act of Union is hardly one generation old; the Union has been subjected to violent stresses and strains from within and is being subjected to others from without. In her present stage of political and cultural immaturity it is too much to expect perfection, and it is surprising that she has achieved as much as she has. Powerful influences within her, as well as others from without, are working towards a solution of her problems. But when 12,000,000 people of four different cultural origins, speaking a dozen different languages, and on every rung of the ladder of literacy and civilization, must live together in amity, solutions are not easily found.

OSCAR DAVID DA FONSECA WOLLHEIM

Dr. Wollheim's forbears were Germans on his father's side who came to South Africa as 1820 settlers, and Dutch on his mother's side traceable as far back as 1652. He was born in 1904 at Stellenbosch, and educated at the University of Cape Town where he took his B.A. degree in 1928 with Nederlands and Afrikaans as major subjects. In 1938 he obtained his Ph.D. for a thesis on Teaching.

Most of Dr. Wollheim's experience has been gained in teaching posts in various schools catering for poor children, at the Wesley Training College, Cape Town, a college for Coloured teachers, and at the W.T. Welsh High School for Natives at East London, a school he founded and of which he was the Principal for twelve years, during which time he saw it grow to be the largest high school in the city.

Dr. Wollheim has travelled extensively in Europe, taught in the London County Council Schools, and in Adult Education Clubs in Surrey. He is now Warden of the Cape Flats Distress Association, an organization performing useful service in the improvement of conditions for the poor, mainly of the Coloured community.

CHAPTER IX

Political Institutions

MARK FIENNES PRESTWICH

IT is not proposed in this chapter to consider the Union of South Africa in relation to the British Commonwealth of Nations, of which it is a part, but solely to give some account of its political institutions and its political life as a self-governing State. Such an account must necessarily be brief because of limitations of space, and being brief it must be somewhat general. That fact makes a warning pertinent at the outset. A brief and general description is apt to suggest to the reader an even greater similarity between the political principles and practices of Britain and South Africa than actually exists. The resemblances are indeed numerous and exceedingly important. The Queen is the formal and titular Head of each State. The Legislature in each is bi-cameral, and in each alike the preponderant part in legislation is played by the Lower House. The active political Executive in each is a Cabinet consisting, regularly in South Africa and almost invariably in Britain, of members of the Legislature, and in each country alike the Cabinet is in fact the initiating, energizing, directing element in government. The various constitutional conventions which determine the actual working of the Cabinet system are, with rare exceptions, much the same in both Britain and South Africa. There are striking resemblances between the party systems of the two countries; there is in each the same trend towards a two-party system (perhaps less decisively so in South Africa) in the sense that, however many smaller parties may actually exist, the political scene is normally dominated by two great parties, and the party struggle is in effect (as it is not, for example, in France and many other European democracies) a clear-cut conflict between Government and Opposition. In each country the relations between the political Executive and the public service are very similar, whilst the relations between the Judiciary on the one hand and the Legislature and Executive on the other are virtually identical. Such numerous and striking similarities in the most essential particulars of government render it all the more necessary to keep continually in mind the dictum which André Siegfried applied to another Dominion, that though English forms may be established ' we must not forget that they are almost always animated by a new spirit.'[1]

Perhaps to no country whose political institutions are largely modelled on those of Britain is this generalization more applicable than to South Africa. For these English institutions and practices have been transplanted into an environment strikingly different in almost every respect from that in which they originally grew. As in other Dominions, the social structure of the European population and its social attitudes differ considerably from those of Britain. Class distinctions, for example, with the European population are, on the whole, less clearly defined than in England; there is little sense of social hierarchy, and there has never been anything that could properly be called a ' ruling class.'[2] These circumstances have certainly affected the political life of South Africa, as of other Dominions. Of greater significance for South African political life is the fact that the European population is divided into two roughly equal sections which are spiritually the heirs of different political traditions. There is the section (it includes many of Afrikaans descent) which inherits the English constitutional tradition; there is the section (almost exclusively consisting of Afrikaners) which derives its political spirit from the Boer Republics of the last century. The effect of this division, to some extent on the political forms of South Africa and still more on the spirit by which they are animated, appears to be much greater than the effect of the division between British and French on the political life of Canada. Unquestionably, however, the circumstance of greatest consequence for both the form and spirit of the South

[1] Brady, *Democracy in the Dominions*, 1947, p. 263. The work contains a valuable account of South African institutions and policies.

[2] That is to say, within the European population. From one point of view, of course, the European population collectively may be regarded as constituting a ' ruling class ' *vis-à-vis* the non-Europeans.

African policy was, and is, the extremely complicated racial structure of the total body of the inhabitants. The racial structure of South African society is dealt with elsewhere in this work; our concern is solely with its effects on political attitudes and institutions. The fact that those who possess citizen rights in the fullest sense—what Aristotle called the ' *politeuma* '[1]—form a comparatively small white minority dominating a much larger non-European majority, itself of varied racial composition and living on many different levels of civilization, has manifestly had a far-reaching effect on the actual forms and institutions of government. It has still more affected the political spirit of South Africa. If a large part of the White population has, in essentials, the outlook of a *Herrenvolk*, most of the rest have something of the mental attitudes that we associate with an oligarchy sharply and clearly distinguished from the unprivileged sections of the community—if, indeed, we can properly speak of the South African community at all.

The broad framework of the existing system of government in South Africa was devised by delegates from the four colonies, Cape Colony, Natal, the Orange River Colony and the Transvaal, and passed into law, without alteration, by the Imperial Parliament in 1909, coming into operation in May 1910. The four colonies, whose association in a legislative union brought South Africa as a single political entity into being, all possessed the same form of government at that time, but their respective backgrounds of constitutional experiences were very different. These differences were not without effect on the form of government created for the Union of South Africa; some consideration of the earlier constitutional history of the four colonies is therefore necessary.

The oldest of the four was, of course, the Cape Colony. There is little that is noteworthy, from the point of view of modern South African government, in its institutions under the rule of the Dutch East India Company. It is sufficient to note that an almost unlimited authority was exercised by the officials of the Company, and that the participation of the local European population in government was narrowly circumscribed. British rule in the Cape did not at first introduce any essential change. During the first period of British rule from 1795 to 1803, and

[1] In one of the several senses in which he uses the word.

again from the beginning of the second period of British rule in 1806 down to 1824, the Governor appointed by the British Crown was, in effect, an absolute ruler. A change in the system came in 1825, when an advisory council was appointed to assist the Governor. At first it consisted only of officials, who were not in any sense representative of the population of the Cape. It combined legislative and executive functions, but it had no control over finance; only the Governor, who presided, could initiate legislation, and its authority was explicitly subordinated to that of the British Government. Nor was the Governor in any way bound by the opinion of the majority of his Council, and he was empowered to suspend any member if he thought it in the public interest to do so. On the other hand, before acting in important matters he was bound to communicate with his Council, and if he took it upon himself to reject the advice of the majority, or if he suspended a member, he was compelled to satisfy the Secretary of State for the Colonies as to his reasons for doing so.

In 1827, two non-official members were added to this purely advisory body, but they too, like the official members, were nominated. The system was radically amended in 1834, when two councils were instituted, an Executive Council of five officials and a Legislative Council of the same five officials together with five non-official members selected by the Governor from the wealthier merchants and landowners resident in the Colony. (The official members were increased to six in 1840, the unofficial members to six in 1848.) A not insignificant change was that the public was allowed to attend the discussions of the new Legislative Council. The new system did not work smoothly. It fell far short of that degree of self-government which the colonists were increasingly coming to desire; there was friction between the Governor and the members of the Council; the attempt by the Council to carry out certain policies of the British Government which were unpopular in the Cape caused the majority of the colonists to lose all confidence in it. A period of discord was brought to an end when genuine representative government was established in 1853.

Under the Cape of Good Hope Constitution Ordinance[1] a

[1] See Eybers, *Select Constitutional Documents Illustrating South African History,* 1795-1910, pp. 45-55, for details of the new constitution.

legislature of the Governor and two elective Houses, the Legislative Council[1] or Upper House and the Legislative Assembly, was set up. The financial qualifications for the franchise were fairly low, and did not require the ownership of fixed property; there was no discrimination on grounds of colour, though the vote was, of course, limited to males. Nor was there any literacy test for the franchise. Under these liberal provisions, a high proportion of the adult male population of the Colony was entitled to registration. Subject to certain obvious exceptions, which excluded for example bankrupts and office-holders, all who were entitled to vote were eligible for election to the Assembly. On the other hand, the qualifications for eligibility to the Legislative Council were set fairly high; members had to be not less than thirty years of age and to possess unencumbered fixed property worth £2,000, or property including movable property to a total value of £4,000, over and above all debts. The principle of representation was territorial for both Houses alike. For the Assembly, the unit was the electoral district returning two members; for the Council, the whole Colony was divided into two great constituencies, the western division returning eight members and the eastern seven. This arrangement was made, of course, in recognition of the somewhat divergent interests and character of the eastern and western halves of the Colony. Minority interests were safeguarded by a system of cumulative voting for members of the Council and for the four representatives of Cape Town in the Assembly.

The Parliament thus established had power to make laws for 'the peace, welfare, and good government' of the Colony, subject to its inability to impair the prerogative of the Crown, to the power of the Crown to disallow any Act within two years, and to the instructions given to the Governor to reserve Bills of certain classes for consideration of the Government of the United Kingdom. On the whole, however, the authority granted to the Cape Parliament was such and was so exercised, that very wide powers of self-government were placed in the hands of the enfranchised inhabitants of the country. 'The ultimate sovereignty of the Crown in Parliament over the Colony remained

---

[1] Of this House, there were fifteen elected members, but a non-elected officer, the Chief Justice, presided over it and was a full member.

unimpaired, but the era of direct Legislation for internal affairs by prerogative instruments was at an end.'[1]

One or two more features of the new constitution call for brief mention. The Executive was not made in any way responsible to the Legislative Houses. The Governor might propose laws, and had the sole right to recommend appropriations of the public revenue, such recommendations to be made to the Assembly. He might return Bills to either House with amendments which he recommended; he might give his assent to Bills in the name of the Crown, or at his discretion refuse it, and he might reserve a Bill (and in some instances had to do so) for the signification of the Royal pleasure. A considerable part of the revenue was reserved to him for expenditure on certain purposes without any specific Parliamentary appropriation. Certain executive officials enjoyed the right to participate in the discussions of either House, and even to bring forward motions, but did not enjoy the power to vote in the Legislature. The right has had some effect on the powers of the modern South African Cabinet Minister.

The Legislative Council under the constitution of 1853 was far from being an insignificant body. Its legislative authority was broadly concurrent with that of the Assembly. It had no power to initiate money bills, but since it was an elected body it was deemed safe to permit it to amend as well as to reject such bills, and the power was used with some freedom. So likewise, at any rate at first, was its general right to reject or amend other legislation sent up to it by the Assembly; it is said, in the first ten years of its existence, to have amended or rejected nearly half the Bills so submitted to it.[2]

This system of government, representative but not in the technical sense responsible, led to friction between the Executive and Legislature, and the British Government itself was anxious on various grounds to bestow on the colonists more autonomy and therefore more responsibility in the ordinary colloquial sense in the determination of their own affairs. Thus in 1872 responsible government (in the technical sense), with the full approval of Britain, was instituted in the Cape Colony by a

[1] *Cambridge History of the British Empire*, Vol. VIII, p. 378.
[2] Kilpin, *The Parliament of the Cape*, p. 87.

measure enabling certain executive officials to be members of one or other of the Houses of the Legislature. In effect, this established a cabinet system broadly similar to that of Britain. Henceforward, subject to certain limitations inherent in the Cape Colony's status as a dependency, the effective direction of the internal affairs of the Colony was in the hands of a group of members of the Legislature administering the several departments of State, who owed their position to the confidence of the Legislature and who were normally expected to resign when that confidence was withdrawn. The principal conventions of Cabinet rule in Britain were henceforth observed in the Cape Colony.

The system of government which exists in contemporary South Africa owes much to the Cape. When Union came in 1910, responsible government as it existed in the Cape was the principal model for the constitution of the new country. The Union's parliamentary tradition has its deepest roots in the Cape Colony.

Little need be said about the constitutional evolution of the Colony of Natal. From the time when it was raised to the status of a separate colony by the Charter of 1856, there was a considerable representative element in the government of Natal, twelve of the sixteen members of the Legislative Council being elected on a broad franchise based on a comparatively low financial qualification. The right to vote was not confined to persons of European descent, but the financial qualification, comparatively low as it was, in effect confined it almost entirely to them. Demands for full responsible government were pressed early, but the concession was retarded by many difficulties, chief among them the numerical preponderance of the Native population over the European settlers and the complicated problems of Natal's relations with the rest of South Africa. The presence, towards the end of the century, of a growing Indian population added to the complexity of these difficulties. When full responsible government came in 1893 (somewhat prematurely, in the opinion of some historians) a rather wider discretionary power was left to the Governor than was usual when responsible government was established in a British colony. Nevertheless in most matters of concern to the White population, it was the policy of Ministers chosen from and dependent on the support of the Legislature that usually in the end prevailed. Between 1893 and the Union of 1910, a vigorous parliamentary life had insufficient time to become well established in Natal, and political parties had not so developed a character as in the Cape. Perhaps the main contribution of the constitutional experience of colonial Natal to the government of the Union is to be found in certain powers of the Executive with regard to the Native population. Thus, for example, from the very early years of British rule in Natal the Lieutenant-Governor, later the Governor, had special and far-reaching powers over the Native population as ' Supreme Chief,' a position inherited by the Governor-General of the Union to-day. In 1897, when Zululand was annexed to Natal, the Governor-in-Council was given powers to legislate for that territory by proclamation during a period of eighteen months, which may be regarded as a precedent for some of the wide powers possessed by the Governor-General-in-Council to-day to legislate by proclamation for the Natives.

If the constitutional histories of the Cape Colony and colonial Natal represent variations on the theme of British political principles and practices, a very different and more purely indigenous tradition is represented by the ' Trekker Republics,' the Orange Free State and the South African Republic (the Transvaal). Both had written constitutions, that of the Orange Free State remarkably clear, concise and adequate to its purpose, that of the Transvaal somewhat confused and ambiguous, deformed by many lacunae and encumbered by much matter not properly in place in a written constitution. That of the Free State was rigid, in that a special procedure was established for constitutional amendment; it is not easy to decide whether that of the Transvaal was intended to be rigid or flexible, but in fact it was treated as completely flexible. Space precludes any detailed examination of the provisions of the two constitutions, but some of their salient features must be briefly noted. Both alike laid great stress on the people as the ultimate source of authority, that of the Transvaal more explicitly than that of the Orange Free State, but both alike considered citizenship as essentially the privilege of a White skin. The Transvaal constitution, indeed, went so far as to state that the people desires to permit no equality between Coloured people and the White inhabitants either in Church or State. So far as the White male inhabitants were concerned, both constitutions were broadly democratic, extending the right to vote very widely and applying the elective principle not merely to the unicameral legislatures which each constitution established, but also to many officials who in other systems of government are commonly appointed rather than elected. The White franchise of the Orange Free State remained liberal throughout its history as a republic, but in the Transvaal the influx, after the gold discoveries of 1885, of many ' Uitlanders ' led to a discrimination between citizens by birth and those who acquired citizenship by naturalization, the latter receiving only somewhat limited franchise rights, and even those, in actual fact, very much at the discretion of the Government. In both constitutions alike, supremacy within the Government lay with the unicameral legislature (Volksraad) alike in legislation and taxation. In each republic there was a President elected for a term of years by the vote of the citizens, and in principle he was subordinate to the Volksraad. He had no right of vote over its acts; his own sphere of authority was limited, and in almost all matters subject to the overriding authority of the Volksraad. In actual fact, whilst in the Orange Free State the supremacy of the Legislature seems to have been maintained, in the Transvaal the President achieved an authoritative influence which no one could have predicted from a mere study of the text of the constitution. The President of each State was, under the two constitutions, assisted—or perhaps in intention restrained—by an Executive Council. In the Free State, the majority of members was elected by the Volksraad, the rest consisting of officials appointed by the President and approved by the Volksraad; in the Transvaal, all save one popularly elected official, were elected by the Volksraad. The members of each Executive Council held office for a term of years, and were not necessarily, like the members of a British Cabinet, united in agreement on a common policy.[1]

There is no direct continuity between the constitutions of the two republices and that of modern South Africa, for with their

---

[1] The texts of the two constitutions will be found in Eybers, *Select Constitutional Documents Illustrating South African History*, pp. 285-96 and 362-410. A valuable study of the two constitutions is found in Bryce, *Studies in History and Jurisprudence*, Vol. I, pp. 359-90.

defeat in the Second Boer War each passed through a period of Crown Colony rule to change, the one in 1906 and the other in 1907, as Colonies with responsible government. Nevertheless the indirect influence of their republican constitutions on the political life of the Union of South Africa has been profound. In them, and the spirit which informed them, Afrikaner nationalism finds much of its political inspiration. Their conception of self-government limited to a White community is obviously of decisive importance for the whole structure of modern South African government; it is not too much to say, with Professor Brady, that 'it shapes the character of South African democracy.' Nor has the non-homogeneous character of their Executive Councils been without some influence on the actual workings of the modern South African Cabinet system.

There is some difficulty in a brief and general description of contemporary South African government, because few of the classificatory terms current amongst political scientists can be applied to it without extensive qualification. If, for example, we seek to describe South Africa with convenient brevity as a unitary democratic State with a flexible constitution we shall find that all the adjectives require considerable qualifying explanation. Notwithstanding the Provincial system, to which some attention is given below, South Africa is undoubtedly a unitary State. Yet the Provinces are something more than mere enlarged areas of local government. They have a certain political life of their own and are still to some extent foci of a special loyalty. Their existence does to some extent affect the structure of the central government, as, for example, in the composition of the Senate. There is a policy, not always regarded in practice, that each Province should at least be represented in the Cabinet. Some of the problems and the tensions of the federal State are paralleled to some extent in South Africa. The country *is* a unitary State, but it is so with a difference. Similarly with the flexibility of its constitution. The South Africa Act lays down the general framework of government, though it did not, even in intention, seek to provide a complete constitutional code. The greater part of it has always been completely flexible, subject to amendment by ordinary legislative process, and amendments by such process have been frequent. Certain so-called ' entrenched clauses,' including one to protect the franchise rights of non-Europeans entitled under pre-Union legislation to be on the voters' roll, and one to protect the equal rights of the English and the Afrikaans languages, were, however, rigid in the sense that they could only be amended by a special procedure, namely, that any amending or repealing act must be passed by two-thirds of the total membership of both Houses, meeting in a joint sitting. Contemporary legal opinion seems to be that as a result of the Statute of Westminster (1931) and the Status of the Union Act (1934) that element of rigidity has disappeared. Nevertheless, even if this be so, there can be no doubt that in the opinion of many people there is a moral obligation to respect the original provisions of the South Africa Act for the repeal or amendment of these clauses, and that opinion is supported by some weighty authority. The South African constitution may be technically flexible, but parts of the instrument on which it is based have, to the political conscience of a large part of the people, something of the semi-sacrosanct character of a Fundamental Law.[1] More obvious, of course, are the reservations which we must make in calling South Africa a democracy. With regard to the White population alone, it may no doubt be properly so-called in one of the generally accepted senses of that much-abused word, but if we consider the whole population of the country, the term must seem inapplicable in any sense. A country in which the great majority of the population, though not wholly rightless, has no political rights and does not always enjoy the same civil rights as the White citizens, is not a democracy in the European or American sense. Perhaps, though with manifest differences, its nearest analogies are to be found in some of the democracies of classical antiquity. Unitary? Flexible? Democratic? The South African constitution is, in a sense, all these, but so much qualification is required in using these terms that to apply them does not greatly assist the understanding of South African government. Unfortunately, the practical consequence is that any real understanding demands acquaintance with considerably more constitutional detail than can be incorporated in this sketch.

The legislative power of the Union of South Africa is vested

[1] See p. 28, footnote 2.

in the Queen (represented in South Africa by a Governor-General, who is now appointed by the Queen on the advice of the Union Cabinet and who exercises most, though not all, of the Royal Prerogative in the Union) and in two Legislative chambers. The more numerous body (now somewhat over 150 members), the Lower House or Legislative Assembly, is in fact the more important. Its members, who must be Europeans, are chosen in single-member constituencies by direct vote of the electors for a maximum period of five years, though the House may be dissolved before that time; it must meet in session at least once every year. The franchise was originally in each of the four Provinces of the Union what it had been in them when they were distinct colonies; subsequent amendments have created what is virtually universal franchise for European adults. In the Cape Province there are still, in virtue of the old franchise, a number of Coloured voters on the common electoral roll, though the amendment extending votes to women did not include Coloured women. The Representation of the Natives Act, passed by a two-thirds majority of the two Houses in 1936, removed such Natives as were entitled to vote in the Cape from the common roll, and permitted them to elect three European representatives of their own who have the same Parliamentary standing as other members of the Assembly, except that they hold office for five years, irrespective of any dissolution. Natives elsewhere have no representatives in the Assembly. Such Indians in Natal as were before 1946 entitled to be registered as voters were also removed from the common roll by legislation of that year and granted special representation, but with the subsequent repeal of Part II of the Asiatic Land Tenure and Representation of Indians Act these provisions, which never came into effect, fell away, and such few Indians as qualify under the old Natal franchise are now entitled to register on the common roll. The law makes provision for the regular re-delimitation of the constituencies in which the common or general franchise is exercised. The method of delimitation is believed somewhat to favour the rural areas at the expense of the urban, a fact not without significance for South African policies, though this discrimination is less marked to-day than it once was.

The House of Assembly is presided over by a Speaker elected

from themselves by the members. Though the reputation of South African Speakers for impartiality is justly high, they are less sublimely detached from party than the Speakers of the British House of Commons. The South African Speaker is often opposed in his own constituency, and he does not consider it improper, even outside election times, to deliver political addresses. The rules of procedure in the House are based on those of the old Cape Assembly and are broadly similar to those of the House of Commons. Parliamentary privilege, which has a statutory basis, includes the essental freedom of speech and debate in Parliament, and such freedom may not be questioned in any Court or place outside Parliament; Parliamentary privilege is not, however, in all respects quite so extensive as in Britain.

The Upper House or Senate is more complicated in its composition. Its core resides in the eight members chosen for a maximum period of ten years in each of the four Provinces by electoral colleges consisting of the members of the Assembly and the Provincial Councillors for that Province, the election being made by a system of proportional representation. The equal representation of four unequal Provinces shows an approach to a practice common in federal states; the system of proportional representation was no doubt designed to protect minorities in a State whose European population is not homogeneous. In addition to the elected Senators, there are eight Senators nominated by the Governor-General-in-Council (in effect by the Cabinet), half of them for their real or alleged knowledge of the ' reasonable wants ' of the coloured races of South Africa. Since 1926, the Senate may be dissolved within 120 days of any dissolution of the Assembly, and in such an event the nominated Senators must also vacate their seats. Finally, in 1936, four Senators were added who are elected in four areas by the Natives, by a complicated system of indirect election which varies considerably in the different areas.[1] Such Senators hold their seats for five years notwithstanding any dissolution. All Senators alike must be of European descent, and must have certain qualifications as to age, property, and period of residence within the Union.

It appears to have been intended that the Senate should be freer from party attachments than the Assembly, and that its

[1] See also note on South-West Africa on p. 130.

composition should render it less amenable to the control of the Cabinet than the Assembly has become. The intention has not been realized. Party is as strong an influence in the Upper as in the Lower House, and at any rate since 1926 a government which is strong in the Assembly is likely to be strong in the Senate too. The Senators representing the Natives, however, do bring to the Senate an element of comparative independence, and some have been men of marked ability which has displayed itself not only in matters where Native interests are concerned. On the whole, however, the Senate has been shunned by the abler politicians, and its rôle in government has not been a very weighty one. It has no special powers, such as those of the Senate of the United States or the Senate of the Third Republic in France. It may initiate legislation, though it may not initiate Bills to appropriate revenue or impose taxes. It may reject or amend Bills sent up to it from the Lower House, but it may not amend money Bills (or clauses in other Bills which incidentally impose taxation) though it may reject them outright. These restrictions do much to limit the power of the Senate. The complaint is often heard that the Government (which in South Africa as in most other countries to-day originates by far the greater part of legislation) does not sufficiently often introduce Bills into the Senate in the first instance, where they could be thoroughly discussed and therefore perhaps dealt with more briefly afterwards by the Lower House. Instead, the Senate finds itself increasingly in the position of having to deal all too hastily with a mass of legislation sent up to it from the Assembly towards the end of a Parliamentary session. Thus if it has largely lost its utility as a check, it has not been permitted to acquire utility as a means of relieving the Assembly of some of its work. Comparatively weak as the Senate is, it would nevertheless be unwise to regard it as insignificant. But both the convenience of Cabinets and the traditions of the Boer Republics are inimical to a Second Chamber with real powers, and some fears have been expressed for the continued existence of the Senate.

Though ordinarily the two Houses deliberate separately, and a Bill must pass through each separately to become law, provision is made for two kinds of joint sitting. One is to resolve a deadlock between the Houses. If the Senate rejects a money Bill, the

Governor-General may call a joint sitting within the same session, and if the Senate amends or rejects ordinary legislation, and no agreement between the two Houses is reached in the next session, the Governor-General may call such a joint sitting in that session. At such a joint sitting, the contentious measure is passed if a majority of the combined membership present votes in favour of it. The other kind of joint sitting is that which the South Africa Act ordains as necessary for the repeal or amendment of the ' entrenched clauses ' of the Act, and at such a joint sitting a two-thirds majority of the total number of members of both Houses, whether or not present and voting, is required for the passage of the proposal. Joint sittings of this latter kind may fall into desuetude if the view prevails that the ' entrenched clauses ' no longer require any special procedure for amendment.[1]

The Crown, represented in practice by the Governor-General, is, as remarked above, a constituent part of the legislative authority of South Africa. No Bill approved by both Houses of Parliament therefore becomes law until it has received the Governor-General's assent.[2] Though he is entitled to withhold such assent, and though he may return Bills to Parliament with proposals for amendment, these reports are of little or no practical significance. It appears to be the recognized practice that he will be guided in this matter by the advice of the Ministers, and as little or no legislation is passed by Parliament which is not initiated or at least approved by them, the Governor-General's assent has in actuality become virtually automatic. The rôles of the Governor-General and of the Senate being in the legislative process what they are, it is normally the case that whatever measure is passed by the House of Assembly becomes law.

The executive government of the Union is vested in the Crown, which in practice has come to mean in the Governor-General. The South Africa Act, indeed, merely states that the Crown may be represented in South Africa by a Governor-General, but it

[1] See p. 28, footnote 2.

[2] No reference is made to the right, and what was in certain cases the obligation, of the Governor-General to reserve Bills in order that the Queen's pleasure should be taken, since this sketch is concerned only with the internal government of the Union considered as an independent state, and not with its position as a member of the Commonwealth. The reserving power was in any case abolished, except in one particular, by the Status of the Union Act, 1934.

PLATE X

A. BLOEMFONTEIN, CAPITAL OF THE ORANGE FREE STATE.

B. THE RAADSAAL, BLOEMFONTEIN.
Once the Parliament House of the old Free State Republic, it is now the Provincial
Council Headquarters.

[To face page 118.

PLATE XI

One of the Peaks of the Drakensberg Range.

has always been so represented, and it is assumed that it always will be. Many provisions in the Union constitution vest certain powers in the Governor-General; others vest powers in the Governor-General-in-Council. In practice the distinction is slight. One Union Statute goes so far as to define the term Governor-General as meaning ' the Officer for the time being administering the Government of the Union acting by and with the advice of the Executive Council thereof unless the context otherwise requires.' For most practical purposes, acts of the Governor-General are acts of the Executive Council over which he presides.

Theoretically the Executive Council consists of persons whom the Governor-General summons to it, who take a prescribed oath, and who hold office during his pleasure. A clause in the South Africa Act prescribes that officers administering departments of State shall be the Queen's Ministers for the Union and shall be members of the Executive Council. On the basis of this clause, the Executive Council has become in practice something very different from its theoretical nature. Though former Ministers in principle belong to it, its meetings in practice are attended only by the Ministers for the time being. Thus the Cabinet, as the collective body of Ministers is called, and the Executive Council are virtually identical in fact, and the acts of the Governor-General-in-Council are in effect acts of the Cabinet. Thus effective executive authority in the Union is in the hands of a Cabinet of Ministers.

In its general character and in the numerous conventions which regulate its working, the Union Cabinet broadly resembles its counterparts in the United Kingdom and in the other Dominions. In one or two respects it diverges somewhat from the former. Thus, for example, the doctrine of ministerial responsibility is statutory, and not simply a matter of convention, in that the Status of the Union Act declares that any reference to the Queen in that Act or in the South African Act shall be deemed to refer to the Queen acting on the advice of her Ministers of State for the Union, except where otherwise expressly stated or necessarily implied. Again, the number of Ministers is prescribed by law[1] and not left as in Britain to the

[1] Originally ten, subsequently enlarged to eleven and twelve and recently (1950) to fourteen.

discretion of the Prime Minister constructing his Cabinet. A consequence of this legal limitation, and the great reluctance that has been shown to enlarge the Cabinet considerably in any of the amendments to the law prescribing the number of Ministers, is that there are more departments of State than there are Ministers, since in the Union as elsewhere modern political problems have led to an increase of governmental activity. Thus it is common for a single Minister to hold more than one port-folio—indeed, it has not been uncommon for a single Minister to hold three at the same time. The results for administration have not been altogether happy, but perhaps the worst result has been that overburdened Ministers have tended to pay rather less attention than some consider desirable to their Parliamentary as distinct from their administrative duties. Furthermore, as the number of Ministers is so small, all are members of the Cabinet, which is not of course the case in Britain, and there are no Under-Secretaries to act as assistant Ministers. That Ministers must be members of Parliament is prescribed by the South Africa Act.[1] A minor divergence from British usage is that Ministers may speak in either House, though a Minister may vote only in the House of which he is a member.

But these legal divergences from British usage are less signifi-cant than some which have no legal basis but arise naturally from South African conditions. It has already been noted, for example, that there is a tendency, not indeed always operative, to impart a certain federal character to the Cabinet by including at least one Minister from each Province. Perhaps that tendency is now passing away; the present Cabinet does not exemplify it. A more striking instance of divergence from the British norm is the rather weaker hold of the doctrine of Cabinet unanimity on South African governmental practice. Many instances could be quoted from the history of the Union. Shortly after Union, General Hertzog expressed views on immigration and bilingualism in sharp conflict with those of the Cabinet of which he was, and for a time continued to be, a member. A similar situation arose in the case of Mr. Tielman Roos in 1925, and Mr. J. H. Hofmeyr

---

[1] No Minister may hold office for more than three months unless he is or becomes a member of either House. The great majority are, or become, members of the Assembly.

in 1936 spoke and voted against the Native Representation Bill sponsored by the Government to which he belonged. In 1939, after the collapse of General Hertzog's Government, members of the Smuts Cabinet who had served in the preceding Ministry attacked former colleagues for measures for which, on a strict interpretation of collective responsibility, they themselves shared responsibility,[1] whilst it is well known that later there were open divergences between Mr. Havenga and his colleagues on one or two fundamentally important matters of policy. This negligence of a principle generally regarded as so important for the Cabinet system in the true sense of the word is not pushed to extremes, but it is sufficiently marked to suggest that in this respect South African Cabinets have resembled those of France rather than of Britain. It may in fact be attributed to the fact that a considerable number of South African Cabinets have been coalition governments, but perhaps it is due even more to the traditions of the Boer Republics, with their loosely organized Executive Councils, the members of which were not expected to be united in pursuit of a common policy. In this connection it is noteworthy that a large proportion of South African Cabinet Ministers, including all Prime Ministers before Dr. Malan, have come from the territories formerly governed by the Boer Republics.

Nevertheless, in most essentials the Cabinet system in South Africa bears more resemblance to that of Britain than to any other. If the Cabinet is not seldom based on the support of a coalition, this circumstance has not produced the results which it has helped to produce in France and many other European countries. South African Cabinets have on the whole been stable, and their expectation of life is reasonably high. Their relation to Parliament is, as in Britain, on the whole one of mastery. The Prime Minister's right to advise a dissolution of Parliament, on which advice the Governor-General will normally act, has operated as in Britain to strengthen the ascendancy of the Cabinet over the Legislature. Taxation and appropriation of revenue must be recommended by the Execu-

---

[1] Perhaps their silence whilst serving under General Hertzog may be regarded as indicating deference for the principle of Cabinet unanimity, but their subsequent attack on the measures of former colleagues shows that they regarded these measures as acts of individuals rather than acts for which the Cabinet was collectively responsible.

tive. The rather frequent use of special Parliamentary committees on public Bills has not in practice restricted the legislative initiative of the Cabinet; there is no analogy in South African Parliamentary life to the special rôle of the committee system in some European Legislatures. The tendency, in South Africa as in Britain, has been to enlarge the responsibility of the Cabinet for initiating legislation on public matters. Comparatively few private members' Bills become law. Private members, indeed, especially when they are in opposition, are apt to complain of the excessive dominance of the Cabinet. There are some grounds for their complaints; more than one administration, especially perhaps the one at present in office, have shown an inclination to limit Parliamentary discussion by a rather free application of such devices as the closure and the guillotine.

The preponderant rôle which the Cabinet in practice plays in the legislative process is assisted, in South Africa, by the comparative brevity of Parliamentary sessions, which leaves little time for the discussion of Bills brought forward by private members. It is assisted also, as in Britain, by the workings of the party system. There are several political parties in South Africa, and there are also other political organizations which are active in the country though they have no status in Parliament, such as the Ossewa Brandwag, the Broederbond, and more recently the Torch Commando. Parties as such are dealt with elsewhere in this work; it is sufficient for the purpose of this chapter to note that notwithstanding the existence of several parties there is a deep underlying trend towards a two-party system. The larger parties at any rate are commonly as firmly disciplined as those of Britain, and Ministers are commonly leaders of one or other of the larger parties. Party caucuses play much the same rôle in each country; party managers have little to learn from anybody of the arts of their kind. A show of independence by a member of the Assembly or of the Senate (save in the case of one representing the Natives) is probably as rare to-day in South Africa as in Britain. There are few members (save again in the case of those representing the Natives) who have no definite attachment to a political party. The electoral process usually works in such a way as to produce, if not an absolute majority for one party, at least the possibility of a durable and cohesive coalition in which one party is dominant. Thus control of the Assembly by the Cabinet is normally firm and easily maintained.

There has been in the Union the same marked tendency as in Britain to delegate law-making powers to Ministers. Many Acts, especially some carried through Parliament by the recent Government, confer very wide discretionary powers on Ministers, often to the extent of allowing them to override the normal right and liberties of individuals by administrative action for which they are answerable to nobody. A special feature of the authority of the Executive in South Africa is the very wide powers exercised by the Governor-General, or the Governor-General-in-Council, over the Native population, powers which include those which he exercises in Natal as Supreme Chief. It is impossible in a brief sketch to particularize these varied powers. They may even permit him to repeal or amend by proclamation Acts of Parliament affecting Natives. All these powers are in actuality exercised by Ministers, since they are invariably exercised on their advice.

No account of the Executive in South Africa, however brief, can omit some mention of the public service. Its relations with other branches of government are broadly the same in South Africa as in Britain. It is distributed into various divisions, including inter alia an administrative and a clerical division, but they have, on the whole, a less rigid character than those of Britain. The Public Service Commission, consisting of three members appointed by the Governor-General (in fact on the advice of Ministers) for five years and eligible for reappointment, exercises various functions, of which the most important are that of recommending appointments and promotions, that of recommending reorganization and readjustment in the public service, that of recommending regulations for the service under the Public Service and Pensions Act, and that of inquiring into and recommending action in the case of serious misconduct. If its recommendations are not accepted, it must lay the facts before Parliament. The system appears to work moderately well, but complaints have been heard in the past that there has been a tendency to appoint good party men to vacancies in the Commission, and there have been instances of a Minister's making appointments to the public service over the head of the Commission.

Members of the public service enjoy a reasonable security of tenure, and South Africa has not as yet experienced the bane of a political public service, though appointments to important posts in it—including one recent example—have sometimes been made on the ground that the person appointed was in sympathy with the policy of the Minister concerned with the department to which the appointment was made. Yet it is disquieting to observe that there are some—in the United Party as well as in the Nationalist Party—who openly call for a public service of that particular political complexion which appeals to them. On the whole, however, the public service has been un-political, free from corruption and prepared loyally to carry out the policy of whatever government is in power. The criticism is sometimes heard that its standard of ability is not sufficiently high. It is beyond question that it contains many very able members, but the comparatively low qualification required for entrance into the clerical division, from which promotions to the administrative division are commonly made, does perhaps operate to keep the general level of ability a little lower than it need be. The recommendation of an earlier Commission of Inquiry that its members should be recruited by competitive examination has not been adopted; instead, the possession of the matriculation certificate is the principal qualification for entrance into the clerical grade.

Although generally detached from political activity, the public service is not quite so ' anonymous ' a body as its British counterpart. Highly placed public servants make occasional public appearances, at the opening of conferences and the like, and although on such occasions they avoid politics in the strict sense, they do sometimes make pronouncements on policy. It has also become quite a fashion in South Africa for a retiring head of a department of the public service to express himself with considerable frankness on matters of public importance.

The judicial system in South Africa presents few features that call for special remark. It is fully centralized. The Supreme Court of South Africa operates through provincial, and some local, divisions, but all are parts of one body. There is an

Appellate Division which hears appeals from the whole country, and its jurisdiction, incidentally, extends to Southern Rhodesia. Until 1948 there was no provision for appeal to the Appellate Division in criminal cases on questions of fact. Now, by leave of the court of trial, appeal on the facts and the sentence may be made. Jurisdiction in petty cases is exercised by Magistrates' Courts. There are certain courts with jurisdiction only in Native cases.

Judges are appointed by the Governor-General-in-Council, and their remuneration must not be diminished during their period of office. They can be removed only on an address presented by both Houses of Parliament in the same session praying for such removal on the ground of incapacity or mis-behaviour. They retire from office, however, at the age of seventy. No special qualifications are prescribed by law for appointment to the judicial Bench, but a convention as rigid as the same convention in England insists that appointments shall be made from qualified advocates. The South African Bench has always included notable figures, and taken as a whole it is as independent as any Judiciary in the world. The magisterial system presents some analogies with the judicial arrangements of certain countries on the European Continent, in that magistrates are paid officers of the public service. Their powers and duties are prescribed by Statute and are both judicial and administra-tive. It is more especially in the country districts that a heavy administrative burden falls upon them. Some believe that this combination of judicial and administrative functions, almost unavoidable in earlier days in South Africa, is undesirable to-day. The criticism has sometimes been heard that magistrates, being paid public officials, are liable to be influenced in the discharge of their judicial duties by the known views of the Minister of Justice, to whose department they belong.

The jury system does not operate so extensively in South Africa as in Britain. The grand jury (which no longer survives in Britain) has never existed here; the civil jury was abolished in 1927, and in criminal cases an accused person has been able since 1917 to elect for trial by a judge and assessors without a jury. From the beginning of the first World War, and the dis-turbances on the Rand in 1922, the Government has enjoyed rather wide powers of setting up special courts for the trial without benefit of the jury system of certain offences against the State.

It may be noted that South African courts must enforce whatever legislation has been passed by the two Houses and duly received the Governor-General's assent. They have no power to question the validity of such a law. The institution of judicial review does not exist amongst us. At one time such an assertion would have required reservations. So long as the Union Legislature was not permitted to pass laws repugnant to United Kingdom Legislation in terms of the Colonial Laws Validity Act of 1865, South African courts had a right and a duty to examine the validity of some statutes. It has also been much discussed whether they would in fact accept as valid any law amending the ' entrenched clauses ' without observation of the special procedure described above. Present indications appear to be that they would, but in view of the uncertainty of the position we should perhaps provisionally qualify the assertion made at the beginning of this paragraph, though it is certainly true in general.[1]

The Provincial system of the Union is unique. Territorially, the four Provinces of the Cape, the Transvaal, Natal and the Orange Free State represent the four former colonies which came together to form the Union of South Africa. Each Province is governed for certain purposes by an Administrator, an Executive Committee and a Provincial Council. The Administrator, who is one of the most important figures in the South African political system (some, indeed, would say next in importance only to a Minister) is appointed by the Union Government for a period of five years, and he is removable[2] only by the Union Government, which also pays his salary. He sits in the Provincial Council but does not vote therein. He is, however, both member and chairman of the Executive Committee, and here he has both a deliberative and a casting vote. The Executive Committee consists of four members, apart from the Administrator, elected by the Provincial Council by a method

---

[1] See p. 28, footnote 2.

[2] Reasons must be assigned and communicated to Parliament within a week, if Parliament is in session, otherwise within a week of the commencement of the next session.

of proportional representation. These need not be members of the Provincial Council; they are all allowed to participate in its discussions, though they may only vote if they are Provincial Councillors. The members of the Executive Committee are not necessarily in agreement on a common policy, and they are not in the technical sense responsible to the Provincial Council. Where (as sometimes happens) there is a standing deadlock in the Committee, the Administrator's power may be very great. The Provincial Council consists of as many members as the Province has Parliamentary representatives, with a minimum, however, of twenty-five. It is elected by the same electors as exercise the Parliamentary suffrage. A Council continues in being for five years, and cannot be dissolved save by process of time. It seems to have been originally expected that Provincial Government would not be affected by party; the expectation has proved vain.

The sphere of action of the Provincial Governments is comparatively limited but not unimportant. A complete list of the matters which fall under their control need not be given here. It is sufficient to note that, inter alia, they exercise an extensive authority in many social services, such as poor relief, the administration of various public amenties, many of the public health services, and elementary and secondary but not higher and technical education. They also supervise local government in the strict sense. They have powers to raise revenue from sources specified in an act of 1945.

Provincial government is unquestionably subordinate to the national government, a circumstance sufficient in itself to exclude South Africa from the category of federal States. Ordinances of the Provincial Council have no validity unless they receive the approval of the Governor-General-in-Council—in effect, that is, of the Cabinet. The Courts will pronounce invalid any Provincial Ordinance[1] which conflicts with the law of the Union. The Administrator, though he is commonly a man who belongs to the Province over which he is set, and although he is expected to advocate its interests, is primarily an agent of the national Government, and as such he is expected to render it a certain obedience and to discharge such tasks as it may impose on

[1] The name given to a legislative measure passed by a Provincial Council.

him. The powers of the Provinces may be enlarged or diminished by Acts of the Union Parliament, and such an Act may always override Provincial Ordinances. The Provinces lack many essential organs of autonomous government: there is no Provincial judiciary, Provincial police, or distinct Provincial public service.[1] Finally, despite powers to raise revenue, the Provinces have never been able to avoid financial dependence on the Central Government. It is easy to criticise the Provincial system. The Provinces, varying as they do in area, population and wealth, are not ideally efficient units of administration. Many administrative anomalies arise from the distribution of functions between the Provinces and the Central Government. Relations between them are often uneasy. Within the scheme of Provincial Government itself, there is abundant scope for conflict and even deadlock between the three organs. Yet whatever indictment may be drawn against them, the Provinces do on the whole represent real units to which regional sentiment attaches. It may be that the time will come when in their present form they can be dispensed with. Even if that time arrives, it may still be necessary in a country of the size and varied character of South Africa to retain units of administration intermediate between local government and the central Government. Meanwhile, the Provinces for all their deficiencies serve a valuable purpose in a country so varied, alike in population and in outlook, as South Africa.

It will not have escaped the reader's attention that the greater part of the non-European, and more especially the Native population, is, to adopt a phrase of Mr. Gladstone, outside 'the pale of the constitution.' We have seen that the Coloured voters of the Cape and the Indian voters of Natal are included in the common electoral roll for the election of members of the Assembly and therefore of the Provincial Councils of their Provinces, but their women are not, like European women, enfranchised, and the old pre-Union qualifications, still prescribed for them, exclude many of them from the franchise. An old law of the Natal Colony, whilst not directly denying the vote to all Natives as such, has effectively deprived them of the

---

[1] There is a single public service for both Provincial and national administrations, with free transfer from one to the other.

suffrage in Natal. We have noted that some provision is made for the representation by Europeans of Cape Natives in the Assembly[1] and of Natives in the Senate, but again the electoral basis of such representation is very far from being broad and democratic. These limited provisions are, as regards the Natives, supplemented by some rather confused and stumbling attempts to give them some voice in their own government. For example there is—or rather was—the Natives' Representative Council, consisting of eight official (and therefore European) members, four Natives nominated by the Governor-General and twelve Natives elected, on a complicated system of indirect election, by very limited electoral colleges. Its functions were solely to deliberate on matters of interest to Natives and on matters referred to it by the Government, and to advise the Minister of Native Affairs therein. An important judgment in 1947 laid down that the Minister was not obliged to refer to the Council for its discussion and opinions all proposed legislation which might affect the interests of Natives. In fact, the advice of the Natives' Representative Council was very often not sought, and, even if it were sought and given, was often not acted upon. In 1949, the Government announced its intention of abolishing the Council. In various Native areas in some parts of the country, there are certain Councils and Boards, on which European officials sit with Natives directly or indirectly elected by the Native inhabitants. Their functions are wholly confined to the sphere of local government, for which they have certain limited financial powers. The extent of their functions, however, varies in different regions. In addition to these bodies, the Governor-General may, under an Act of 1920, establish local councils consisting exclusively of Natives in areas set apart for Natives. They are usually partly nominated and partly elected, and their functions, also, fall exclusively within the sphere of local government. Some twenty-eight such councils have been established, and they are said to work well. Finally, under an Act of 1945, an urban local authority is empowered to set up a Native Advisory Board for every Native location or village under its control. Such, in broad outline, are the attempts which have

[1] They are also represented by two members (who must of course be Europeans) in the Cape Provincial Council.

been made to reconcile the aspirations of some of the Natives for a voice in matters of concern to them with the almost universal conviction of European South Africans that the Native is not ripe for self-government and that European predominance must be maintained.

A Note on South-West Africa

It was thought not desirable to complicate the account of the South African Parliament by referring in the body of the text to the arrangements made in 1949 to give South-West Africa representation in the Union Legislature. Under these arrangements, South-West Africa, which the Union administers as a mandated territory, is represented in the Union Parliament by six elected representatives in the House of Assembly and by four Senators. Two of the Senators are elected, and two nominated by the Governor-General, one of these latter on account of his acquaintance with Native affairs and aspirations. These representatives enjoy the same rights and privileges as Union Members of Parliament. In South-West Africa itself an administration similar to that of a Province is established under the Act of 1949. There is, however, a significant difference. In place of the Provincial Council found in the four Provinces, there is an elected Assembly with much wider powers, including almost complete control of South-West Africa's finances. The Union Parliament is to have no power to extend any tax or charge or duty imposed on the people of the Union to the territory of South-West Africa. These fiscal provisions of the Act of 1949 are to be repealed or amended only on the request of the Assembly of South-West Africa. Thus the Act of 1949 adds considerably to the complexity of South Africa's political institutions, and raises some technical questions of great interest to constitutional lawyers and political scientists.

MARK FIENNES PRESTWICH

M. F. Prestwich was born in Lancashire in 1911 and graduated in History at St. John's College, Cambridge. In 1937 he was appointed Lecturer in the Natal University College, as it was then called, and in 1944 he became Senior Lecturer in History and Political Science. He has broadcast a number of talks.

CHAPTER X

Political Parties and Trends

RENE DE VILLIERS

OF South Africa's 12,646,375 inhabitants, only the Europeans, numbering approximately 2,643,000, and Coloured people in the Cape Province, about 924,000, can qualify for the vote. The 8,535,000 Africans are directly represented by three representatives out of 159 in the Lower House, elected by the Cape on a communal basis, and four out of 50 in the Upper House, one for Natal, one for the Free State and Transvaal, and two for the Cape Province—also communally elected. The Coloured have been on the common roll with the Europeans for the past century in the Cape. The Indians, on the other hand, numbering about 365,524, have no franchise in Natal, where 85 per cent of them live, nor in the Transvaal. In the Cape Colony they have the vote on a basis similar to that of other enfranchised groups. They are excluded by law from residence in the fourth Province—the Orange Free State.

Ever since the formation of the Nationalist Party by General Hertzog, two years after the birth of the Union (1910), political allegiances have very largely revolved round the relationships between the English and the Afrikaans-speaking sections of the community which are in the ratio of 2 to 3. Botha and Smuts, at the Union, adopted a policy of conciliation between the two white sections on the basis of a constitutionally independent South Africa within the framework of the British Empire, and concentrated on the establishment of a South African patriotism founded upon an acceptance of the existing racial position. With this purpose in view, they founded the South African Party, which drew its support from both the English and Afrikaans-speaking sections. Botha's policy, which had the enthusiastic backing of General Smuts, was to build a South African nation through the coalescence of the diverse white racial elements in the country. Englishman and Afrikaner were to be treated on a basis of equality.

General Hertzog, more sensitive to Afrikaner sentiment, feared that the Afrikaans-speaking section might occupy a position of inferiority and lose their identity as a nation. He argued that until the Afrikaner had social, economic and cultural equality with the English-speaking section, there could never be real co-operation or real conciliation. The English-speaking groups occupied the dominating position not only in the public service of the country at the time, but in mining, commerce, finance and industry, while the Afrikaner, generally speaking, had to be content with second place in well nigh every sphere except the political. General Hertzog, therefore, decided that the Afrikaner was to use his numerical majority over the English-speaking section to obtain cultural, social and economic equality. The symbolism of the British section was to be swept away, the Afrikaans language was to be accepted as the equal of English in all spheres of life, the adverse balance against the Afrikaner in the public service was to be removed, and Afrikaner ' poor whiteism' was to be combated by the concession of privileges financed by the national Treasury as much as by general economic reform, in which the emphasis was to be placed more and more on industrial development to provide employment and investment opportunities for South Africans and South African capital. To achieve these ideals he forced a break with Botha and formed the National Party in 1912. He preached what came to be known as ' Hertzog's two-stream policy': the development of the two race groups side by side until the two could face each other as equals; after that they could merge to form one powerful South African stream.

General Smuts's attitude may best be explained by quoting from Roberts and Trollip, *The South African Opposition* (Longmans). ' He looked forward to higher integrations of human society . . . .what he perhaps did not see was the middle distance of the next generation or so . . . . He found it difficult to understand that the Nationalist creed, which had been exorcised for him by three years of war, might in others have been confirmed and strengthened by that conflict, and that his people might not reach his standpoint until more than one generation had left the Jameson raid and the concentration camps behind them.'

However, by 1933, the two leaders, who had fought each other bitterly inside and outside Parliament throughout the previous 21 years, decided that the time had arrived when Hertzog's two-stream policy and Smuts' one-stream policy could fruitfully merge. A severe economic crisis, followed by a demand that South Africa leave the gold standard, and an insistent public clamour for political change following on two decades of sterile political squabbling on racial lines, gave the two men the opportunity of merging. Their leadership was threatened by the bid for power made by Tielman Roos, an Appeal Court judge, who proposed to form a central party on the ' off the gold standard ' issue. The fusion of the Nationalist and South African Parties into the United Party, with General Hertzog as Prime Minister and General Smuts as his deputy, foiled this plan. At the same time South Africa went off the gold standard and Tielman Roos, who had forced the issue was left without political or judicial standing. (He had resigned as a judge to enter politics.)

In spite of stresses and strains, the United Party combination ruled South Africa until 1939, when it split on the issue of whether South Africa should enter the war against Nazi Germany. General Smuts took the majority of the United Party members of Parliament with him, and General Hertzog resigned as Prime Minister, and subsequently as a member of the United Party. A rapprochement between him and Dr. Malan, the leader of a group of Nationalists who had refused to follow General Hertzog into the United Party six years earlier, led to the formation of the Re-united Nationalist Party early in 1940.

But from the first it was obvious that the alliance would be an uneasy one. General Hertzog stood for moderation and race co-operation, Dr. Malan's followers emphasised an independent republic as a national ideal. The break came 14 months later, at a Free State congress of the Re-United Nationalist Party, and it came, significantly enough, on the Party's attitude to the English-speaking section of the community. General Hertzog declared that he would not be associated with a party which was not prepared to guarantee equality of status and political rights

PLATE XII

GOVERNMENT HOUSE, CAPE TOWN.

PLATE XIII

CLOUDS OVER TABLE MOUNTAIN.

to both sections of the European population : one race should not and could not dominate the other. His opponents in the party denied that they had any intention of depriving the English-speaking section of their rights, but failed to satisfy General Hertzog, who resigned his leadership and membership of the party. He took with him a relatively small group of supporters who some months later founded the Afrikaner Party, which took its stand on a political philosophy that has since come to be known as Hertzogism. Hertzog himself, however, took no active part in the new party's activities, resigned as a member of Parliament, and remained in semi-retirement until his death in 1942.

Against the Hertzogism of the Afrikaner Party Dr. Malan preached an Afrikaner Nationalism best defined by the term Krugerism. This aimed at the creation of an Afrikaner republic on the basis of Afrikaner national unity and the gradual assimilation of the English-speaking section, and their admission to civic rights on that basis. In other words, the new Nationalist Party planned to Afrikanerise the non-Afrikaans elements. Roberts and Trollip put it this way : ' Hertzog's policy in the twenties, they (the Malan Nationalists) freely acknowledged, had been necessary and right, but now he was refusing to follow that policy to its logical conclusion. Of what use was it, Malan could argue, to nurse the traditions, encourage the cultural efflorescence and protect the status of the Afrikaner, if, as soon as these great aims were secured, the purity of the Afrikaner way of life was to be watered down by admixture with a civilization and a people certainly alien to it in spirit, and probably also hostile ? In their view, the Afrikaner should aim at monopolizing important appointments, he should deliberately strengthen himself in social groups where hitherto he had been weak; he should understand the principle of bilingualism to mean, not that each citizen should be required to speak both languages, but that every man should be protected against having to speak a language that was not his own. In short, they embarked upon a line of policy which, if followed to its logical conclusion, would have led to racial exclusivism and frank isolationism, ramifying into every aspect of society; and this they did, partly because they believed it necessary in the interests of national purity;

partly because they honestly believed that the English would
never get rid of those ties of sentiment which, by holding them
fast to England, made them incapable of becoming good South
Africans.'

In other words, the Nationalists believed in an Afrikaner
rather than a South African unity—a unity in which the average
English-speaking South African could have no real part unless
he identified himself absolutely with Nationalist aspirations. The
goal was to be an Afrikaner-dominated republic, free from the
Commonwealth, with Afrikaner ideology affecting every branch
of the policy. General Hertzog's brand of broad and tolerant
nationalism now that equality had been achieved had little
popular appeal and in the general election of 1943, the Afrikaner
Party suffered a crushing defeat, not one of its members being
returned to Parliament. Dr. Malan's Nationalist Party, on the
other hand, increased its representation from 25 to 45 seats out
of 153, and so remained the official opposition to the United
Party led by General Smuts. Five years later, to the astonish-
ment of its supporters and the consternation of its opponents, the
Nationalist Party won no fewer than 70 seats at the general
election. In addition it helped its war-time adversary, the
Afrikaner Party, which, under the leadership of General
Hertzog's disciple, Mr. Havenga, had formed an election agreement with Dr. Malan's party, primarily on the colour issue, to
win nine seats. Dr. Malan and Mr. Havenga were able to form
a coalition government with a majority of five over all other
parties. Mr. Havenga and his eight followers were very much
the junior partners in this combination, and Afrikaner nationalism, as distinct from South African nationalism, or Hertzogism,
ruled the Union of South Africa for the first time.

What, it may be asked, are the objectives of Afrikaner
Nationalism in its new form? The most unambiguous reply to
this question has come from one of the young intellectuals in
the Party, Professor A. I. Malan, M.P. In August, 1949, he
stated the Party's attitude in these terms: 'The whole question
of the driving power of Nationalism reduces to that of survival.
This point is cardinal. He who fails to recognize the fundamental fact that the Afrikaner is fanatically determined to
survive as a European race, has failed to grasp the most ele-

mentary fact of South African politics. Why this fanaticism? Let us consider the facts, and maybe the reason will become clear. The Continent of Africa contains roughly 130 million people, of whom four million are White, and among these Europeans there is only one single distinct and separate nation, the Afrikaner nation. For better or for worse this tiny nation has decided that, in spite of the overwhelming preponderance of the black and coloured races, it is going to survive as a European nation at the Southern extremity of Africa . . . . The objective of Afrikaner Nationalism is primarily the perpetuation of European culture in a limited corner of the vast Continent of Africa . . . . Hegemony of the Afrikaans group is not one of the ideals of the National Party,' Professor Malan continues, ' that is very definite. However, if the Afrikaner finds that only by achieving hegemony will it be possible for him to survive, he will in no way hesitate to try and attain hegemony, not as an ideal in itself but as a necessary tool towards his ideal of survival.'

Professor Malan goes on to explain that there is a difference between the attitude of the Afrikaner and of the English-speaking South African towards this question of survival. The English-speaking South African, he maintains, will also try to preserve his European blood. But if this entails too much effort and too much sacrifice, he would under certain circumstances be prepared to capitulate. After all, there would still be at least 40 millions of his race in Britain who would carry on his way of life. The case of the Afrikaner, however, is quite different. ' He belongs to a small nation in whom the youthful consciousness of his manly power has only just awakened, and who looks towards an eager future. If he should vanish from the stage, who remains to perpetuate his way of life, his culture? . . . . Can it thus be wondered at that, for the Afrikaner, the matter of survival has become an irresistible life force, a veritable obsession?'

Strongly coloured by religious feeling, Afrikaner nationalism rests, to a large extent, on the political philosophy of Calvin. It rejects as too individualistic the liberal philosophy of the nineteenth century, and sees in Nationalism and Liberalism two irreconcilable ways of life. It places the emphasis on the duties of the citizen to the State rather than on his rights, and emphasizes the importance of the State. It professes to be demo-

K 2

cratic, but it excludes all who are not deemed worthy of citizen rights.

The mystical conception of Afrikaner Nationalism is propagated by a super-organization of Afrikanerdom called the Afrikaner Broederbond (Bond of Brothers), a select secret society. One of the most intriguing political problems in South Africa is to try to determine to what extent, if any, the powerful Nationalist Party is ruled or dominated by this secret society. At the time of writing (1950), for instance, it was known that the Nationalist Prime Minister, Dr. Malan, and at least a third or perhaps even a half of his Cabinet, as well as the majority of Nationalist members of Parliament, were members of the Broederbond. The organization dates back to some time after the failure of the 1914 rebellion—brought about by the question of the Union's participation in the war on Britain's side—when a number of Afrikaans-speaking people met and founded a society with the object of establishing an Afrikaner Republic in South Africa. Its membership to-day is only about 3,000, mostly handpicked men in key positions in their own sphere. Up to the time of the fusion of the Nationalists and South African Parties in 1933, the Broederbond was primarily a cultural organization, but then it widened its sphere and adopted the purified Nationalist Party, led by Dr. Malan, as its political instrument.

The Broederbond's declared objectives are : the abolition of inferiority of Afrikaners and their language; strict segregation of all non-Europeans; an end to exploitation of South Africa and its people by ' aliens '; and the Afrikanerization of our public life and our education in the Christian National sense, leaving the internal development of all sections free as long as it does not militate against the State.

The General Secretary of the organization wrote : ' The Afrikaner Broederbond is born from a deep conviction that the Afrikaner nation was planted in this country by God's hand and is destined to remain as a nation with its own character and its own mission.'

When General Smuts was Prime Minister he banned the civil service from membership of the Broederbond. The late General Hertzog also condemned the Bond. Its opponents maintain that the Bond has a staff of experts who work in secret through a large number of subsidiary organizations in the political, the cultural, the economic and the religious spheres.

Up till the second World War, the Nationalist Party represented chiefly the farming community. But this picture changed rapidly after 1940. With industrialization came urbanization, and Afrikaners in their thousands trekked to the towns and cities to become skilled and semi-skilled workers. There emerged Afrikaans urban capitalists (mostly in finance-capital), commercial men and industrialists, professional and academic groups, and urban skilled and semi-skilled groups. There was therefore no longer a simple economic basis to the Party. A large Afrikaans working-class population sprang up on the Witwatersrand, subject to the attractions of city life which tend to dissipate the church and ' volk ' allegiance of the worker. Afrikaners also entered the prosperous business and professional classes. The workers became subject to the teachings of trade unionism and other influences which divide society into worker and employer, rather than race. But there was one point at which all these groups could meet: their common fear of the black majority. The Nationalist Party used this unifying force. A special fund was created to assist the party in spreading its gospel among the organized workers.

With the complication of the social pattern, a rift occurred in the Nationalist Party between the Cape or ' moderate ' wing of the party and the extremists in the Northern provinces (with some support from the Cape). Mr. Strydom and his followers stood resolutely by Krugerism undiluted, while Dr. Malan came to say that he was prepared to postpone the issue of a republic until the people as a whole were ready for it.

Operating on the political periphery were various organizations born in the inter-war period. The chief of these was the Ossewabrandwag, under the leadership of Dr. J. F. J. van Rensburg, a former Union Secretary for Justice, and ex-Administrator of the Orange Free State Province. Born out of the emotions generated by the Great Trek centenary celebrations in 1938, it originally typified and embodied the spirit of revivified militant Afrikaner Nationalism. Under Dr. van Rensburg, however, it was organized as a military hierarchy upon the cell system. In the early days of the war it claimed a very large

membership, alleged to be close on 300,000, and acts of sabotage
were committed by some of its extremist elements. As the
second World War drew to a close and authoritarian regimes
lost their appeal, the Ossewabrandwag membership dwindled
rapidly, until in 1950 it was of very little consequence. It
settled down to more ' constitutional ' methods, and threw in its
lot with Mr. Havenga's Afrikaner Party, much to the annoyance
of staunch Nationalists, who saw the organization as a potential
threat to the Party's political hegemony. The Ossewabrandwag's
ideology is perhaps best summed up in these two official quota-
tions :

' The Ossewabrandwag is Afrikanerdom's protection against
Parliamentarianism. The Ossewabrandwag is not an imitation.
It is a movement which has assumed different names in various
countries. In Italy it was called Fascism; in Germany National
Socialism; in Spain Falangism, and in South Africa the
Ossewabrandwag.' (Statement by Dr. van Rensburg, March,
1942.)

' To-day we must go forward to the modern idea of the
organic unity of the volk with the responsibility of service and
the authority of leadership as essential components.' (Professor
L. J. du Plessis, member of the Great Council of the Ossewabrandwag.)

Another pseudo-Fascist organization which arose during the
war, and was still functioning, although on a reduced scale in
1950, was the New Order, under the leadership of Mr. Oswald
Pirow, a Cabinet Minister in General Hertzog's Governments of
the 1930's. Mr. Pirow propagated Afrikaner Nationalism with
a colouring of Nazi ideology. The organization of the New
Order was also based on the cell system.

Then there was the so-called Grey Shirt movement, born in
Hitler's heyday, and known for some years as the South African
National Socialist Party, which was officially dissolved in 1950.
Anti-Semitism was the main ingredient of its programme. It
lent what support it had to the Nationalist Party. When it broke
up, the head of the organization, always referred to as ' the
leader,' urged his followers to join the Nationalist Party.

Both the Ossewabrandwag and the New Order envisaged a
system in which citizenship shall be graded in various classes,

full rights being accorded only to those who give unqualified support to the movement, and only, of course, to Europeans.

Opposed to the Nationalist Party of Dr. Malan, stands the almost equally strong United Party, led by General Smuts from 1939 onwards. The United Party was the lineal successor of the South African Party established by General Botha in 1910, led by him till his death in 1919, and then by General Smuts till its fusion with the Nationalist Party of General Hertzog in 1933. Taking its stand on the broad basis of South African nationhood, the United Party drew its support from both main European race-groups, although after the general election of 1948, its Parliamentary representation was largely confined to urban areas, and the great majority of its supporters were English-speaking. At the same time, leadership remained in the hands of Afrikaans-speaking Parliamentarians, and its policy was always designed to make an equal appeal to rural and urban voters, English-speaking as well as Afrikaans-speaking.

The Party stood for South Africa's close association and co-operation with the other members of the British Commonwealth of Nations, at the same time emphasizing South Africa's sovereign independence and freedom of action under all circumstances. It believed in the ideals of international co-operation, and welcomed the establishment of the United Nations. At the same time, it shared with the Nationalist Party a determination not to allow ' interference ' in what it believed to be the domestic affairs of South Africa.

In the economic sphere the Party's policy of industrial and mining development, plus a measure of protection for young industries, did not differ fundamentally from that of the Nationalist Party—a fact which occasionally brought it under heavy fire from the more Leftist elements in the country. A shrewd political observer, and former Member of Parliament, Mr. D. B. Molteno, Q.C., once pointed out that the obvious answer to the attempts of the Nationalist Party to utilize Afrikaner sentiment for the purpose of penetration into the fields of banking, business, finance, and labour organization, was to broaden the basis of South African economy by developing the consuming and producing capacity of the 80 per cent of the people who are not Europeans. The Nationalist onslaught on the

economic front depended largely on the mobilization of the
national sentiment of about ten per cent of the total population
of South Africa, he argued, and as such it was bound to be
narrowly based.

' There is a section of the United Party and its supporters to
whom all this is clear,' Mr. Molteno wrote. ' They see the
futility and sterility of a society and economy based on the frustration of the potential producing and consuming powers of the
non-European peoples and of a party system based on a struggle
for the control of this narrowly-based society and economy. Yet
this is not the viewpoint of the Party leaders and organizers. On
the basis of our present economy,' Mr. Molteno adds, ' the
United Party has no function other than the purely negative one
of repelling the Nationalist onslaught upon key positions. That
onslaught is being conducted mainly outside the Parliamentary
field. Yet partly because they fear for their inherited privileges
as white men, partly because the United Party, although it has
lost its meaning and function, still represents a great political
vested interest, the reactionary wing, together with most of the
Party leaders and organizers, persist in the attempt to beat the
Nationalists at their own game.'

This contradiction in the philosophy of the United Party
resulted in industrialists being told that the Party stood for the
development and mobilization of the country's entire human
and material resources and for the abolition of the industrial
colour bar, while white labour was told that it stood for the
maintenance of the colour bar. The Platteland, again, was
told that the United Party stood for cheap Black labour and
high agricultural prices, while consumers were told that it stood
for an enlarged domestic market and low food prices.

These inherent contradictions, combined with inept administration, in some spheres of Government, contributed largely to
the downfall of the United Party Government in 1948.

There has been no Liberal Party as such in South Africa,[1] but
there were scattered groups of people who call themselves
Liberals. The unofficial leader of these people was the Right
Honourable Jan H. Hofmeyr, Deputy Prime Minister in the
Smuts Administration, whose death at the age of 54 in 1948,

---

[1] A Liberal Party was in fact formed on 9 May, 1953.

was a bitter blow to Liberal hopes. Broadly speaking, Mr. Hofmeyr and those who share his views stood for the gradual extension of political rights to non-Europeans, and believed in equality of opportunity for all races. He strenuously opposed the 1936 Native legislation, fought the Indian Pegging Act of 1943 which placed restriction on the purchase and ownership of property by Indians in the Province of Natal; and he agreed to the Asiatic Land Tenure and India Representation Act of 1946 only because, as a quid pro quo for the land restriction clauses taken over from the Pegging Act, the measure provided for political representation (since repealed) for the Indians of Natal in their own Provincial Council as well as in Parliament. He said at the time, moreover, that this was just the beginning : some voice in local government would have to be accorded to the Indian people.

Mr. Hofmeyr also maintained that at some stage or other the non-European groups should have direct representation in Parliament and provincial government by members of their own races. He claimed that political segregation was impossible without territorial and economic segregation. His emphasis was always on development of the non-European peoples, on raising their standards of living and assuring them of greater facilities for self-betterment.

Mr. Hofmeyr was accused of plotting the overthrow of ' white civilization.' The 1948 election was fought and won by the Nationalists very largely on the exploitation of Mr. Hofmeyr's views. A section of the United Party plotted more or less openly to get him thrown out of the Party after the election, maintaining that the Party would never return to popular favour while he was a member of it. After his death Hofmeyr's personal policy was propagated, unofficially, by his followers inside and outside the United Party. Men like Senator Edgar Brookes spoke in true Hofmeyrian accents, but liberalism could not by any stretch of imagination be regarded as a political force of any consequence.

To some extent the party membership of a South African voter is determined by his attitude towards the position of non-Europeans in the community. Generally speaking, the Europeans of South Africa could be divided into three categories :

firstly, those who maintain that the non-European must not be given political rights except in areas specifically reserved for his occupation. Otherwise, they argue, the European will sooner or later find himself swamped, outvoted and dominated by the coloured races. Secondly, those taking their stand on the 1936 'settlement' of the Native problem, which removed Natives in the Cape Province from the common electoral roll and put them on a communal roll, at the same time giving them the right to elect three Europeans to represent them in the House of Assembly. Provision was also made for a measure of indirect representation in the Upper House for the Natives of Natal (one representative), of the Transvaal and Free State (one) and of the Cape (two). These two groups, which very roughly represented the viewpoints of the Nationalist and United Parties respectively in the early 1950's, are of more or less equal strength in the land.

The third group, which included members of the United Party as well as some in the Labour Party and a body of politically homeless voters, maintained that the political representation which the Natives were given in 1936 was inadequate, that sooner or later the non-European would have to come on to the common roll with the European; that representation, to be effective, must be direct; and generally, that political segregation was impossible as long as there was not territorial or economic segregation. This group has always been in a decided minority in South Africa.

After the general election of 1948, the Nationalist Party took its stand on the basis of 'apartheid,' or separation of the races. According to a Party commission appointed in 1947, apartheid was 'based on the Christian principles of justice and reasonableness,' and stood in contrast to the policy of 'equality, which advocates equal rights within the same political structures for all civilized and educated persons, irrespective of race or colour, and the gradual granting of the franchise to non-Europeans as they become qualified to make use of democratic rights.' The aim of 'apartheid' was the maintenance and protection of the European population as a 'pure white race,' the maintenance and protection of the indigenous racial groups as 'separate communities within their own areas, and the stimulation of national pride, self-respect and mutual respect among the various races.'

The Nationalist Party believed that the policy of the country had to be so planned that it would eventually promote the ideal of complete segregation in a natural way. It stood for a policy of developing the Native Reserves so that they would become 'the true fatherland of the Natives,' and believed the drift of Natives to urban areas to be 'dangerous.' It did not want the number of detribalized Natives to increase. All Natives living in European areas had to be placed in separate residential zones, and their concentration in the urban areas had to be curbed. The Native in the urban areas should be regarded as a 'visitor' who 'can never be entitled to any political or equal social rights with Europeans.' Natives from the rural areas and Reserves would be allowed to enter European areas only as temporary workers, and must return to their homes regularly on the expiration of their service contracts. The principle of separation would be carried out in factories, industries and workshops so far as is practically possible.

The Party was opposed to the organization of Natives in trade unions, and advocated a system whereby the State, as guardian, would take care of Native interests. The Nationalist Party in 1948 expressed itself in favour of abolishing the indirect representation of Natives in the House of Assembly and undertook also to change the representation in the Senate. Over and above four European Senators appointed by the Government in terms of the South Africa Act by virtue of their special knowledge of Native matters, the Natives would be represented in the Senate by four European Senators, elected by the various Native Councils. These seven Senators would form a standing permanent committee on Native matters. The Native representatives, however, would not be able to vote in (1) votes of confidence in a Government, (2) a declaration of war and (3) a change in the political rights of non-Europeans. The Party favoured the abolition of the Natives' Representative Council and hoped to establish a system of local administration in Native areas. In urban areas councils would be established which, however, would never be allowed to develop into independent bodies.

The Nationalist Party also expressed its intention of abolishing the rights of the Cape Coloured community to franchise on the common roll with Europeans, and to replace it by a system

of representation in the Senate, whereby, a European representative would be appointed by the Government because of his
knowledge of Coloured affairs; three Europeans would be
elected to represent the Coloureds in the House of Assembly.
The voting powers of these three representatives would be circumscribed in the same way as those of the Natives in the
Senate. The Nationalist Party proposed that in their own areas
the Coloured community would have their own Councils and
their own public services, which would be managed by themselves within the framework of the existing Councils with higher
authority.

As far as the Indian population is concerned, the Nationalist
Party manifesto of 1948 said that Indians ' are a foreign and
outlandish element which is unassimilable.' They were therefore
to be treated as an immigrant community. No Indian immigrants would be allowed to enter the country and the Party
accepted as the basis of its policy the repatriation of as many
Indians as possible. Those that remained would be strictly
separated from Europeans and other non-European groups,
would not be given any representation in the legislative bodies
of the country, would not be allowed to reside or to own fixed
property in European areas, would have their facilities for
trading outside their own areas, especially in European areas,
drastically curtailed, and would be given fewer and fewer opportunities for trading in Native areas, or locations. In addition
the inter-provincial movement of Indians would be effectively
prevented.

The United Party believed that territorial segregation was
impracticable and undesirable, but was in favour of social
separation and residential segregation in urban areas, and was
also opposed to racial intermixture. It accepted the two million
Natives living in towns and villages on the fringe of European
towns and cities as part of the country's permanent urban
population. Their presence close to the mines and the industries, the United Party argued, was essential for the continued
economic development of the country. (This was in line with
the Party's attitude to industrial development. The mines and
industries need a plentiful supply of labour close at hand.)

As far as political representation of the African people is

concerned, the United Party has consistently taken its stand on the 1936 legislation, and envisaged the development of a greater measure of self-government in the Native Reserves, although such self-government would always be under the jurisdiction of the European Parliament. As far as the urbanized Native population was concerned, the Party envisaged an extension of the system of Native Advisory Boards which would gradually be given more power to regulate life in Native townships. At the same time the Party expressed its intention of extending the scope and powers of the Natives' Representative Council. This body was set up under the Representation of Natives Act of 1936, to secure a channel through which the Government keeps in touch with Native opinion, and had to be consulted before legislation affecting the Native people is enacted. There is nothing in the Act, however, to suggest that the Government is in any way obliged to heed the Council's advice.

The United Party also pledged itself to carry out the main recommendations made by Mr. Justice Fagan and his three fellow-commissioners in the Native Laws Commission Report of 1948. These were, very briefly : the gradual breaking down of the system of migratory labour; the gradual modification of the pass laws, and plans for the better control of life in Native urban areas. The main points of the Fagan Report were the categorical statement that the Natives living in towns and cities must be regarded as an integral part of the urbanized population of the country.

The United Party, however, after the 1948 election which it lost on the Native issue, stressed in its programmes of principles that it stood for ' European leadership and authority ' and recognized the ' factual position ' of ' the differences between Europeans and Natives.' In general, the Party stated, it aims at maintaining and promoting goodwill and understanding in the race relationship ' in the abiding interests of the country as a whole.'

The policy of the United Party in relation to the Coloured people of the Cape was based on the recognition of the special position which they occupy in the multi-racial society of South Africa, and ' of the desirability of raising the standards and improving the living conditions of the Coloured people.' The

United Party held that Coloured people should not be deprived of their existing political rights.

As far as the Indian population was concerned, the United Party found itself in an extremely difficult position. A very strong element in the Party has always been opposed to granting the Indian people any political rights, while the remainder, with the exception of the Liberal wing, were only lukewarm in their support of the franchise provision of the 1946 Act, since repealed.

What, it may well be asked, was the attitude of the Labour Party on the fundamental issue of colour? Did it not adopt a clear and unequivocal line? Paradoxically enough, since its foundation in 1908, the Labour Party constantly bumped its head very hard against colour problems. The result was a series of crises and purges which in 1948 left the Labour Party with six members of Parliament, a shadow of its former self, for it once had 21 representatives in the House and a big share in the Hertzog Pact Government of 1924-1929. In 1946 it was shaken to its foundations by the Indian Bill, over which both its leader, Walter Madeley, and its deputy-leader, M. J. van den Berg, resigned because they objected to political rights being granted to the Indian people.

The other section of the Labour Party maintained that the colour bar in industry was in reality a cheap labour bar, and urged, as a solution to the problem of skilled Native workmen, the slogan of equal pay for equal work. It denied, just as the trade unions did, that if Black and White had to compete for work on that basis, the Black man would stand little chance of obtaining it because of the colour prejudice of the mass of employers.

In the political sphere the new Labour Party accepted the principles of limited political rights being granted to the non-Europeans. It believed that a federal political system in South Africa would become inevitable, and envisaged a full measure of home rule for the non-European people. In the meantime it believed that it was essential to arrange for progressive representation of non-Europeans in terms of a franchise conditioned by educational qualifications. It also urged that Natives in European areas be given a political voice in local government by the extension of local government to non-European townships, and by indirect representation from freely elected non-European township councils to Municipal councils, in the same way as indirect representation was given them in Parliament and in the Senate. It never, however, advanced this part of its programme with much vigour or enthusiasm, as the white worker in general fears that he may be ousted by the black man.

On broader issues the Labour Party declared socialism to be its objective, that is, ' the ownership and control by the people of the means whereby they live, and of the nation's financial and currency system.' But, as is so often the fate of social democratic parties, the South African Labour Party, has constantly come under fire from Left as well as from Right. It should be noted here that the South African Labour Party is not composed of ' workers ' as a whole, but consists in the main of skilled European artisans. Some years ago the leader of the small but not uninfluential Communist Party, Bill Andrews, wrote : ' The future of the South African Labour movement is not easy to forecast, but it seems obvious that as long as the great mass of the workers of the country, that is, the non-Europeans, remain outside the ranks, both political and industrial, it cannot function as a dominating factor in the affairs of the country.'

The Communist Party, dissolved in 1950 a few weeks before the Suppression of Communism Act was promulgated, was the only political party which gave membership to non-Europeans on a basis of complete equality and was opposed to any colour bar, political, social or economic. The Communist Party had only one representative in the four Provincial Governments of the country, and only once managed to get one of its members elected to Parliament. At the 1948 general election there were only three Communist Party candidates throughout the country, and all three finished at the bottom of the poll. In November, 1948, the Native electors of the Cape Western constituency elected a Communist to represent them in Parliament. With the outlawing of the Communist Party in South Africa in 1950, it will be impossible for the Party to be represented in Parliament.

At the time of writing South African politics are as fluid as they have ever been, and some re-alignment of forces is thought to be well nigh inevitable. Ever since the Union, the main political battle was between an almost exclusively Afrikaans-speaking group and an English-speaking group supported by a considerable leavening of moderate Afrikaans-speaking voters. Constitutional, political and racial rather than economic considerations characterized the conflict. After the second World War this began to change. A 'new' race element was introduced: it was no longer the relationship between English and Afrikaans that was of paramount importance, but the relationship between the white and the non-white groups. It was this, above all else, that came to determine the White people's political allegiances, either drawing them together or driving them apart.

What does the non-European think of the White man's politics? The great majority of discerning Natives, Indians and Coloureds, saw very little difference in the basic attitudes of the main European political parties to the colour issue. The Natives' Representative Council, for instance, embarked on a policy of non-co-operation with the United Party Government in 1946, which it sustained until and after the election in 1948. It was at the time of the strike of African mineworkers on the Witwatersrand that the Council first decided to adjourn as a protest against the Government's refusal to allow it to debate the strike and the events which led up to it. At the same time it passed a resolution calling upon the Government to repeal all discriminatory legislation, and to give the Natives' Representative Council executive power and a greater measure of authority. The Smuts Government did not accede to these requests, although about a year later General Smuts put forward some tentative proposals for enlarging the Council and increasing its scope and authority. The suggestions had a frigid reception from the African people, who reiterated their demand for citizenship rights, even if limited.

A sense of frustration and hopelessness became more and more evident in the writings and utterances of the African people, culminating in a feeling of deep dismay when the Nationalist Party came to power in the middle of 1948. Similar reactions were shown by the Cape Coloured community, whose spokesmen had threatened an appeal to the United Nations. This was the course which the Indian people of Natal, the Transvaal and the Cape adopted; they prompted India to sponsor their case and ask U.N. to declare that the Government of South Africa was dishonouring its obligations by its discriminatory race policy. This action, significantly enough, had the effect of uniting a very large cross-section of the European community in South Africa against the Indian people. The Europeans maintained—as did their representatives when arguing the case at U.N.—that this was a matter of domestic concern and U.N. had no right to interfere. The South African Indians went further, and for over a year indulged in a passive resistance campaign in Natal, as a result of which hundreds of Indians were gaoled for infringement of the law.

Frequent attempts were made to bring about non-European unity on a political basis in South Africa, but without success, but the Nationalist victory gave a fresh impetus to these attempts. Under the leadership of the African National Congress, and with the support of Left-wing Indian and Coloured organizations, some degree of non-European unity had been achieved by mid-1950, but lack of self-discipline and organization among the Native masses made anything like concerted non-European action almost impossible to achieve. A 'national day of prayer and protest' in June, 1950, called by an ad hoc non-European committee, was a failure. However, the African mineworkers' strike in 1945, when over 60,000 unorganized, unsophisticated and tribalized Natives took part, showed that large scale concerted action is possible.

Not surprisingly, the growing political consciousness of the non-European people and their increasingly insistent demands for basic democratic rights and privileges tended to draw together sections of the European population which had little else in common. So, for instance, during the 1948 elections, there was the curious phenomenon of a purely English-speaking political group led by an ex-Labour M.P., the Rev. C. F. Miles-Cadman, and the Dominion Party, led by the English unilingual Victorian, Colonel C. F. Stallard, K.C., making common cause with the Nationalist and Afrikaner Parties on the colour issue. Neither of these groups secured representation in the new Parliament, although Mr. Cadman was subsequently appointed to the Senate by the Government. Similarly, in the United Party there have always been numbers of people who are

at heart in sympathy with the non-European policy of the
Nationalist Party.[1]

Can South Africa avoid what everyone dreads—a conflict
between White and Black? This is what South Africans are
asking themselves to-day. Is the strong hand of the ruling white
man the safeguard? Or will denial of all political aspirations
precipitate a conflict? The answer to this is the key to all
political trends in the Union of South Africa to-day. It might
be, as someone has said, 'All Union politics are Native affairs.'

R. M. DE VILLIERS

Born Orange Free State, 1910, son of Afrikaans-speaking
parents. Educated Grey College School and Grey University
College, Bloemfontein. Bachelor of Arts, 1930. Subsequently
followed a diploma course in international studies at London
School of Economics, 1934-36.

Became Editor of ' The Forum,' a national political weekly, in
1946, and Editor of ' The Friend ' a daily newspaper published in
the Free State, in 1949.

Contributed a chapter on Bantu politics to the ' Race Relations
Handbook,' published by the South African Institute of Race
Relations in 1948.

---

[1] After the 1953 election, in which the National Party was returned with an
increased majority, the Opposition (United Front) split up, and two new parties
were formed : the Liberal Party (see p. 142) and the Federal Party which aims
at a federation, first of the various parts of the Union of South Africa and then,
rather remotely, of all Southern Africa.

CHAPTER XI

Economic Factors

PROFESSORS JAN GOUDRIAAN and D. G. FRANZSEN

MODERN economic development, in the tradition of Western Capitalism, dates back to the discovery of diamonds at Kimberley and gold on the Witwatersrand in the seventies and eighties of the last century. Before these mineral discoveries, the economy of the Union had been based on the farming industry, with wool as its major product. The natives were then living apart, content with their primitive tribal economy. Little over-seas and local capital had been invested in the Union's economic system before its mining industry got under way.

The expansion of the Union's economy, based on minerals, was largely financed by means of foreign, primarily British, capital. According to S. H. Frankel's estimates in his book *Capital Investment in Africa*, the Union attracted overseas capital to the order of £525 million during the period 1870–1936. The bulk of the capital subscribed for non-governmental enter-prises was invested in mining operations. In later years the Union's secondary industry has also benefited to an increasing extent from the capital inflow from abroad, with a resulting acceleration of the pace of over-all economic development.

The opening up of the Rand mines stimulated development in every direction. Apart from the inflow of capital, the mines attracted European immigrants and ' know-how ' to the Union. Non-Europeans, especially tribal natives, were drawn into the labour market on a big scale. The construction of a railway network, linking up the Rand with the Union's principal ports, a big expansion in the field of urban real estate and municipal enterprises, as well as of industries ancillary to the mines, and a change-over in the system of South African farming from a semi-subsistence to a cash crop basis, so as to cater for the new

internal markets, are among the more direct changes caused by
the impact of a highly-capitalized industry on the pre-gold
' wool economy ' of the Union.

In the twentieth century the rise of industrial production has
been the outstanding feature of the Union's economy. Nature
has not only endowed South Africa with gold and diamonds,
but with the basic mineral prerequisites of an industrial
economy, viz., coal, iron ore and other base minerals. The
Union's coal, at present the cheapest in the world, ensures cheap

TABLE I

Net National Production of the Union, 1911-12 (£000,000)

	1911-12	%
1. Farming and Fishing	21·1	16·1
2. Mining	36·0	27·5
3. Manufacturing	8·9	6·8
4. Wholesale and Retail Trade ...	18·0	13·7
5. Transport...	9·9	7·6
6. Central Government	5·4	4·1
7. Provincial Government	2·4	1·8
8. Local Government	1·5	1·1
9. Rent	11·5	8·8
10. Services	16·2	12·5
Total Net National Income ...	130·9	100

Source : *South African Journal of Economics,* June, 1944.

The national income figures of the Union are now presented
in accordance with a more detailed breakdown. The 1948-49
figures are shown in Table II.

power, in the virtual absence of hydro-electric power potentialities. The State has also adopted a protective attitude towards
local industry during the last three decades. Examples are the
Electricity and Iron and Steel Acts, both passed in the twenties,
which started the career of State-controlled public utilities in the
power and heavy industries, respectively, and tariff protection,
which also dates back to the twenties.

Two major developments in the last two decades, as in the

eighties of the nineteenth century, have been the exploitation of two new gold fields in the ' Far West Rand ' and the Northern part of the Orange Free State.

TABLE II

Net National Production, 1948-49 (£000,000)

I. *Productive Enterprises*

A. *Business*

	Industrial Groups			1948-49
1.	Farming, Forestry, Fishing	...	...	124.2
2.	Mining	...	...	93.0
3.	Manufacturing, private ...	...	...	195.4
4.	Trade and Commerce	...	...	126.6
5.	Transportation ...	...	...	84.0
6.	Liquor and Catering	...	...	15.2
7.	Professions ...	...	...	19.1
8.	Miscellaneous Business :			
	(i) Public ...	...	...	34.4
	(ii) Private ...	...	...	14.7

B. *Home Ownership*

9. Private Dwellings	...	...	...	26.1

II. *Finance, Banking, Insurance* 22.4

III. *Final Consumers*

A. *Public Collective Providers* :

(i) Union Government	...	...	...	36.4
(ii) Provincial Administrations	...	...	33.9
(iii) Local Authorities	...	...	...	16.9
(iv) Education, Control Boards	...	...	3.8

B. *Private Persons* 26.5

Total Geographical Income 872.6
Less Net Income Accruing to Non-Union
Factor of Production 40.9

Net National Income 831.7

In common with other young, developing countries, the rate at which further diversification of the Union's economy takes place will be determined by the speed with which additional capital, also from abroad, can be mobilized. The development of a balanced economy may, however, be handicapped by limiting factors, e.g., lack of adequate water supplies to meet the needs of expanding industries and urban communities. Regional planning is bound to become an increasingly vital issue in the future.

Contemporary Economic Structure

Table 1 presents the Union's net national production, calculated in accordance with the industrial origin approach. Very significant shifts have occurred in respect of the relative importance of the different industries.

A study of the two tables reveals that the secondary and tertiary industries have been making rapid gains at the expense of primary and extractive industries. The percentage contribution of farming dropped from 21 per cent to 14.9 per cent between 1911-12 and 1948-49. The corresponding percentages for mining are 36 per cent and 11.2 per cent, and for manufacturing 9 per cent and 23 per cent.

The occupational distribution of the Union in the year 1936 is shown in Table III. It will be noted that the majority of the natives were engaged in agriculture. In the Native Reserves farming is practically the only occupation. The preliminary figures of the 1946 Census indicate a shift in the occupational distribution, away from farming. The number of persons engaged in manufacturing, services and other tertiary industries has increased considerably, which is what one can expect to happen in a country that is rapidly becoming industrialized and urbanized.

The real national income in the Union has been increasing steadily in the past decades. During the thirties its rate of increase was much faster than that of U.S.A. or Britain, because the Union enjoyed great prosperity after the devaluation of the South African pound in December 1932, whilst many overseas industrial countries were still in the grips of secular stagnation and unemployment. The point is often made by economists in the Union that fluctuations in the country's real income and

TABLE III

Major Occupations of the Various Races in the Union, 1936

Occupations	Europeans 15 years and over		Coloureds 15 years and over		Asiatics 15 years and over		Natives 10 years and over	
	Number 1936	%	Number 1936	%	Number 1936	%	Number 1936	%
Agriculture	181,409	24·84	96,262	34·77	18,056	28·12	3,096,436	73·31
Mining	46,936	6·42	3,370	1·23	862	1·34	393,020	9·31
Industry	132,629	18·15	47,273	17·07	11,438	17·81	213,765	5·06
Transport and Communications...	77,830	10·65	11,497	4·15	1,617	2·52	91,339	2·16
Commercial and Financial ...	119,006	16·29	14,241	5·14	17,263	26·89	6,689	·16
Professional, Entertainment, Sport	124,563	17·05	14,235	5·14	4,069	6·34	21,940	·52
Personal Service	30,528	4·18	72,719	26·26	7,646	11·91	356,270	8·44
Other and Undefined Workers ...	17,660	2·42	17,279	6·24	3,255	5·07	43,931	1·04
	730,561	100·00	276,876	100·00	64,206	100·00	4,223,390	100·00

total employment are much less severe than in overseas countries. The reason for this greater economic stability is the important role played by the gold mining industry in the Union's economy. In depressions the cost of production of the mines drops, but the price of their product remains fixed, so that they can expand operations.

During and since the second World War the Union has not experienced the same rate of increase in nominal and real national income as Britain or the U.S.A., because it already enjoyed more or less full employment at the outbreak of war. Table IV shows the trend since 1937-38.

TABLE IV

Real National Income, Union, 1937-48

Year	Real National Income (£000,000)	Index (1937-38 = 100)
1937-38	374·8	100·0
1938-39	388·2	103·6
1939-40	419·3	111·9
1940-41	442·9	118·2
1941-42	462·6	123·4
1942-43	463·7	123·7
1943-44	480·3	128·1
1944-45	493·6	131·7
1945-46	513·8	137·1
1946-47	502·1	134·0
1947-48	524·5	139·9

Comparisons between the real income per capita in the Union and Western countries cannot be made, because of the heterogeneous composition of the Union's population. A very large percentage of the total population is still living on a primitive subsistence basis. The Native Reserves, containing 3.1 million Natives, have not yet shared in the development of the country on modern lines. The result is that the comparative income figures of the Union submitted by writers such as Colin Clark (in his *Conditions of Economic Progress*) are meaningless, because the different racial groups should be weighted according to their income status in order to arrive at a theoretical population figure which could be used for international comparisons of real income per capita. Unfortunately there are no reliable studies available in regard to the income distribution of the Union according to race. The average income position of the European compares very favourably with the per capita income in other developed or developing countries. The improvement of the income status of the non-Europeans depends on the extent to which the areas set aside for their exclusive occupation, i.e., the Native Reserves, are developed by the introduction of secondary and tertiary industries, and the raising of the wages and productivity of the non-Europeans employed in the European-owned sector of the economy.

More details about the low productivity per man-hour as the basic cause of non-European poverty will be given in the section on labour conditions in the Union. The labour market of this country has been dominated in the past by the ' cheap labour ' fallacy, or, phrased differently, the ' economy of *low* wages.' Capital and skilled labour were in short supply, but untrained, illiterate non-Europeans could be hired at will.

The problem of attaining higher over-all income standards in the Union is complicated, however, by the fact that the majority of the Natives do not share the traditions and *mores* of Western civilization with the European section of the community. They have a fundamentally different outlook on life. Western traits such as acquisitiveness, thrift, foresight and responsibility for the future are lacking. Leisure is more highly prized than the reward of constant toil. The acceptance of the norms of Western society can take place only after the tribal customs of the Reserve natives have fallen away. This is bound to be a gradual development.

Labour Resources of the Union

According to the 1951 Census the Union's population is made up of 2,643,187 Europeans, 365,524 Asiatics, 1,102,323 Coloureds, and 8,535,341 Natives, a total of 12,646,375.

The Union's labour force has only to a limited extent been recruited from Europe. The big reservoir of cheap indigenous labour existing in the Union has discouraged mass emigration of unskilled workers to the Union, and European immigrants are usually persons with some capital of their own, and with professional qualifications or some degree of skill. Unskilled immigrants from Europe would be forced to compete with non-Europeans at mere subsistence wages, and the same dilemma faces the European migrant from the rural areas to the labour market of the cities. There is no niche in the unskilled labour market for the European worker, under present conditions.

Of the 7.8 million Natives in the Union in 1946, 1.7 million were living in the urban areas, and 3 million in the rural areas of the European-owned sector. 40 per cent, i.e., 3.1 million, were living apart in the Native Reserves, i.e., land set aside for the sole occupation of Natives. A labour recruiting service has been established, however, whereby big employers of Native labour, e.g., the gold mining industry (which employs about 300,000, on the average), obtain the services of Natives living in the Reserves and outside the Union for certain contractual periods. The Native recruits return to their homes after a period lasting up to a year, but many return to work for further periods under European employers. Apart from the recruitment of Native workers on an organized basis, there is a constant migration of individual natives and families between the Reserves, farms and cities. The net result is an alarming labour turnover in South African industries, which again explains why the productive output per man-hour of the migrant labourer, who is in most cases without training or experience of regular industrial employment, is low.

The effect of the migratory labour system on the economy of the Native Reserves is serious too. The best manpower of the Reserves is constantly being drained off, and the children and aged persons and women are unable to cope with the task of rehabilitation and development which is necessary to raise the Reserves' Productivity. The age-distribution of the Transkei, one of the Reserves, compared with that of 'European' cities, reveals this state of affairs. 75.2 per cent of the urban Native male population (in the European sector) was between the ages 15 and 45, whereas the corresponding figures for the Transkei was 33.9 per cent. The reverse was true in the case of infants and aged persons.

The Union also attracts native migrants from the British protectorates and other African territories. Although the average wage standard of the Native worker employed in the Union is low, in comparison with European standards, Native wages are much higher in the Union than in the neighbouring states. This differential serves as a powerful migration incentive, and the recruiting bodies which recruit the non-Union Natives for service in the Union do not experience difficulty in getting their full quota of foreign workers. The number of protectorate Natives working in the Union in 1946 was approximately 120,000, and in December 1946 the gold mines which made use of the Labour Recruiting Service were employing 111,898 Natives from Northern and Southern Rhodesia, Nyasaland and Mozambique.

TABLE V

Proportions of European Urban and Rural Families in Different Income Ranges, 1941

Urban Families		Rural Families	
Income Range	% Distribution	Income Range	% Distribution
Under £100	10·0	Under £50	22·9
£100–£199	16·8	£50–£99	22·8
£200–£299	18·2	£100–£149	13·4
£300–£399	19·8	£150–£199	8·8
£400–Over	35·2	£200 +	32·1
Total ...	100·0	Total ...	100·0
Median ...	£324	Median ...	£116

Source : U.G.28, 1945.

Up to the present time the emphasis in the Union's labour market seems to have been on the number of workers available, rather than on the quality of the workers. Thus far capital has been the relatively scarce factor of production in the Union's economy. During and since the second World War the supply of labour has been becoming increasingly inelastic, however, and this may force employers to organize their labour force in such a way that output per worker rises.

Urbanization

The growth of the secondary and tertiary industries of the

Union has been accompanied, as in other industrializing countries, by a progressive shift of population from the rural to urban areas, increased from 65.2 per cent in 1936 to 72.5 per cent in 1946, and the corresponding percentages for non-Europeans were 22.4 per cent and 26 per cent.

The rural areas of the Union have experienced an absolute decline in the number of Europeans. In 1931 708,327 Europeans were enumerated in the rural areas, as against 652,252 in 1946. Apart from this absolute decline, the rural areas lost all their natural increase (122,000 in the period 1936-46) to the cities.

Because of the relative poverty of the rural areas of the Union, the higher *money* income per urban family acts as a migration incentive. Table V shows the distribution of families in urban and rural areas according to different income ranges.

10 per cent of the urban families had incomes of less than £100, and 26 per cent had incomes below £200. 68 per cent of the rural families had incomes below £200. The mean income of rural families was only about one-third of the figure for urban families.

The rapid urbanization process in the Union has caused serious bottlenecks, especially in the field of non-European housing. Between 1936 and 1946 the Native urban population increased by more than 500,000, and many of these newcomers are ' squatting ' in shanty towns on the outskirts of cities like Johannesburg. The presence of these improvised ' townships ' is a serious menace to the health and safety of the established city-dwellers.

Because of their low productivity under the present industrial set-up and the operation of a colour-bar, the Natives receive low wages, so that they are not in a position to afford ' economic ' homes. Although provision is made for funds for sub-economic housing schemes, too ambitious projects of this nature would shoulder the municipal authorities with serious deficits in regard to this item. Various schemes have been mooted to meet the housing crisis. One is that there should be a housing levy on employers of Native labour. Another is that the Natives should be allowed, under European supervision, to be owner-builders, using standardized materials.

The Native Urban Areas Act, originally passed in the twenties, empowered urban authorities to prohibit ' squatting ' of Natives who were without permanent employment or housing, within the municipal boundaries. The rapid industrialization of the European urban areas, especially since the beginning of the second World War, has made it well-nigh impossible for local authorities to deal satisfactory with a problem which can be tackled only on a national scale. This would involve, among other things, the creation of labour exchanges to regulate the flow of Natives to employment centres, and the provision of alternative avenues for the employment of Natives by starting industrial establishments in the Native Reserves, within the framework of well-co-ordinated long-term regional development programmes.

Another long-term problem facing metropolitan areas such as the Rand, Pretoria and the cities-to-be on the Free State goldfields is the shortage of water for residential and industrial needs. The bulk of the water requirements of the abovementioned urban communities are met from the Vaaldam, near Vereeniging. When its potential capacity has been reached (some estimates put the time limit at 1975), the Union would of necessity be forced to adopt a policy of decentralization in respect of its secondary industries. There are well-watered regions, such as Eastern Transvaal, Northern Natal and Transkei, which are at present not industrialized.

From a discussion of the broader issues underlying the Union's economy, we can now turn to a study of some of the features of the Union's primary, secondary and tertiary industries.

The Farming Industry

On account of natural conditions the productivity in South African farming is low, compared with countries abroad. Much can be done, of course, to improve farming methods. Nevertheless, a study of the rainfall and soil potentialities of the Union has shown that it would never be able to support a large scale agricultural industry. About 80 per cent of the total area of the country has a summer rainfall, with 6 dry months in winter, and the rest has a winter rainfall with 6 dry months in summer, with the exception of a very small area where it rains all the year round. Only one-third of the country has an annual rainfall of

TABLE VI

Gross Value of Farming Production (£000,000)

(a) *Agricultural Products* :—   1947-48

1.	Maize	34.1
2.	Wheat	10.6
3.	Kaffircorn	3.2
4.	Winter Cereals	3.2
5.	Potatoes	3.0
6.	Tobacco	4.6
7.	Beans, Peas	1.3
8.	Ground Nuts	3.0
9.	Sunflower seed	1.0
10.	Fresh and Dried Fruit	12.9
11.	Wines	3.7
12.	Vegetables	6.2
13.	Sugar Cane	5.7
14.	Wattle Bark	1.7
15.	Hay, etc.	3.7
16.	Other Agricultural Products	0.5

Total ... 98.4[1]

(b) *Pastoral Products* :—

1.	Wool	19.2
2.	Cattle (slaughter)	19.3
3.	Sheep (slaughter)	8.9
4.	Pigs	4.4
5.	Mohair	0.4
6.	Fresh Milk and Dairy Products ...	20.2
7.	Poultry and Poultry Products ...	4.7
8.	Other Pastoral Products	1.6

Total ... 78.7[1]

Grand Total : Agricultural and Pastoral Products ... 177.1[1]

[1] These figures have now been revised. The 1947-48 revised figure for agricultural products is £103·3 million, pastoral products £78·0 million and the total £181·3 million.

more than 25 inches. Much of the Western and interior parts
of the country are semi-desert. In the non-coastal areas rains,
when they do occur, often come in torrential downpours, and
run off quickly. The threat to the country's top soil on account
of erosion is very serious indeed.

Apart from its low annual rainfall the Union is subject to
periodic droughts, which may last a few years at a time. At
present less than 6 per cent of the total area of the country is
cultivated. The maximum area that can be brought under
cultivation is authoritatively put at 15 per cent. The maximum
area that could be used for irrigation schemes is estimated at one
million morgen. This is less than one per cent of the total area
of occupied farms and agricultural holdings, viz., 103,488,206
morgen (1946 figure).

Climate, vegetation and soil have contributed to make pastoral
production the mainstay of South African farming. The Union
is self-sufficient in pastoral products, and its wool clip already
figured prominently among the Union's exports a century ago.
The vulnerable spot in the Union's farming industry is wheat,
which is the staple food of the European population. Wheat is
produced, in normal years, with the aid of an import duty, but
on balance the Union has been importing as much as 40 per
cent of her wheat requirements. Fortunately the production of
maize, which is the staple food of the Natives, has been adequate
to meet most of the demand, and experiments with new hybrid
varieties hold out the hope of substantial increases in yields per
morgen in future.

The chief products of the farming industry are shown in
Table VI. The calculations are made by the Division of
Economics and Markets, Department of Agriculture.

The most important export products are wool and deciduous
and citrus fruit. The sugar, wattle bark and wine industry also
produce and export surplus.

The trend of farming production in the past decades is re-
vealed by the figures of Table VII.

The figures relate to European and Native production, and
are expressed in terms of producers' prices, i.e., net of marketing
costs.

With 1936-37—1938-39 as base period, the index of the gross

value of all farming products has increased to 275 in 1947-48, and the index of producers' prices of agricultural and pastoral products to 233. This shows that the increase in gross output is also accounted for by an increase in the physical volume of farm products during the war and post-war years.

Structure of the Farming Industry

Farming is carried on in two separate areas, viz., in the ' European sector ,' and in the Native Reserves. In accordance with Acts of 1913 and 1936, certain scheduled areas have been

TABLE VII
Estimated Gross Value of Agricultural and Pastoral Produce
(£000,000)

Season	Total Gross Value of Agricultural Products	Total Gross Value of Pastoral Products incl. Poultry Products	Total Gross Value, Agricultural and Pastoral Products
1910–11	14·6	14·6	29·2
1920–21	24·1	28·5	52·6
1930–31	22·8	21·8	44·6
1940–41	43·1	34·7	77·8
1950–51	—	—	213·0

set aside for exclusive occupation by Natives. Ultimately the area allotted to the Natives will amount to 12 per cent of the total area of the Union, as against 70 per cent which is owned by European farmers. The bulk of the Native Reserves is situated in well-watered areas.

Of the 112,453 European farms and holdings, according to the 1945-46 Agricultural Census, 24,722 had an area exceeding 1,000 morgen apiece and 45,190 an area exceeding 500 morgen per farm. The size of these bigger farms, taken as a whole, can be gauged from the fact that the farms of more than 1,000 morgen each accounted for more than 70 per cent of the area of all farms; the corresponding percentage for farms with a size of above 500 morgen each was 90 per cent. Almost 15 per cent of the total farming area was taken up by farms with an area of more than 10,000 morgen each. (One square mile is approximately 302.4 morgen.)

PLATE XIV

Vineyards in the Paarl Valley, Western Province.

This fertile area was a centre of Huguenot settlement in the late seventeenth century.

[*To face page* 166.

PLATE XV

THE SOUTH AFRICAN IRON AND STEEL CORPORATION (ISCOR) WORKS, PRETORIA.

European farming is carried out on a cash-crop basis, and owners form the predominant group among farm operators, as can be seen from Table VIII.

TABLE VIII

Nature of Tenure, European Farms, 1946

	Number of Farms.	Morgen.
Owned by occupier	77,167	73,751,367
Leased by occupier	23,071	16,216,410
Occupied on share system	6,098	3,911,628
Managed for other persons	6,117	9,608,701

The European-owned farming sector is experiencing an increasing labour shortage, as the non-European farm labourers are attracted to the cities by the higher wages. Mechanization is gaining ground, however, and in 1948 10,822 tractors were imported.

Native farming is still governed by ancient tribal customs, in many cases. In the Transkei arable lands are divided in allotments of about 5 morgen per farm operator. These small holdings militate against the introduction of modern farming practices. Mechanization and the adoption of a new system of farming based on conservation of the natural fertility of the soil are impossible under present conditions. Deep-rooted primitive beliefs, over-crowding of the Reserves, lack of capital and lack of co-operation with the Department of Native Affairs in its attempts to reclaim some of the lands that have been ravaged by erosion make the displacement of the subsistence farming by a new modern system of farming a slow process. The farming production in the Reserves is so low that they are net importers of foodstuffs from the European-owned farming sector. The economy of the Reserves has been a classic example of the Malthusian Law for decades, and the over-population is relieved only by the export of surplus labour to the European labour market.

The Rehabilitation of the Farming Industry

Soil erosion has now become a national problem in the Union. Jacks and Whyte, in their study of soil erosion, entitled

The Rape of the Earth, state that a national catastrophe, due to soil erosion, is perhaps more imminent in the Union than in any other country. Overgrazing, lack of crop-rotation, absence of contour cultivation, and similar malpractices have caused denudation which is especially serious in the Native Reserves.

The Soil Conservation Act of 1946 establishes the machinery for an attack on the problem on a national scale. Scarcity of funds and equipment have hampered the reclamation work, especially in the Native Reserves. The Government Departments concerned are also pushing ahead with agro-economic studies so as to determine the type of farming systems which would ensure the best use of land in the different parts of the country.

Another handicap experienced by South African farming is the prevalence of animal and insect pests. The Department of Agriculture has organized several research institutes to combat these diseases, and the work that is being done at places such as at Onderstepoort Laboratories, Transvaal, is of the highest order. At present the Veterinary Service Division is engaged upon a big campaign against the tsetse fly and nagana in Northern Natal. Helicopters are used in the dusting of the infected areas with D.D.T. and B.H.C.

Marketing and Mortgage Structure of the Farming Industry

In an effort to stabilize prices of farm products, Parliament passed the Marketing Act in 1937. The Control Boards established in terms of this Act advise the Minister of Agriculture and the Cabinet in regard to the prices to be fixed for the current season for the various products controlled, viz., cereals, meat, dairy products, fresh fruit, dried fruit, tobacco and chicory. The prices are determined in most cases in accordance with the cost-plus principle. At present producers have majority representation on the boards.

Over-capitalization is common in the farming industry in the Union. A suggestion has been put forward by the Department of Agriculture that the State-controlled Land and Agricultural Bank, which was started in 1912 for the purpose of making advances to farmers against the security of first mortgage on land, should be changed into a National Mortgage Bank, which should have the monopoly of farm mortgages. This Bank would grant loans based in valuations of farm property drawn up by a 'Bureau of Farm Valuations,' a body which the Department would like to see established at the same time. In this way over-capitalization could be avoided, according to the Department's view.

In 1943 the Land Bank and State Advances Recoveries Office held total farm mortgages of approximately £30 million. The total farm mortgage debt of the Union is estimated at about £100 million. About 70 per cent of the mortgages is thus privately held.

The co-operative movement in South African farming is making rapid progress. In 1939-40 the total business turnover of registered co-operative farming association was £27.9 million, of which £25.0 million was the turnover in respect of farm produce. The rest is accounted for by farming requisites handled and services. In 1947-48 the total turnover was £81.0 million, of which £67.8 million was due to the handling of farm products.

The number of farm co-operatives as at 30th June, 1949, totalled 240, of which only 15 were still organized on an unlimited liability basis. The total membership was 200,027.

Fisheries

The Union has excellent fishing grounds, and the output of the industry has been increasing rapidly. The landings of fish caught by trawlers operated by the deep sea fishing industry in 1948 totalled 85,552,400 lb., valued at £868,597. The Union's fleet of trawlers numbered 40. The bulk of the output of the inshore fisheries in 1948 was made up of about 150 million pounds of pilchards and maasbankers. These fish were canned, and were also used for the production of fish meal and oil, the production of which totalled 20,000 tons and 1,250,000 gallons respectively. About 250,000 soupfin sharks, used in the vitamin oil industry, were caught. The inshore fishing fleet numbered 2,307 boats in 1948.

A ceiling has been put on the exports of crawfish, so as to prevent overfishing. The ceiling quantities are 2 million lbs. per annum for frozen crawfish tails and 4.1 million lbs. for canned crawfish. The whaling industry of the Union is also expanding.

Forestry

The Union's low rainfall makes afforestation in most parts of the country impossible. In 1949 the total afforested area of the Union was 201,715 morgen. The total area of forest reserves was 1,669,913 morgen, and a long term afforestation programme is being pursued by the Union Government.

In 1949 the yield of timber from Government forest reserves and plantations was 26.3 million cubic feet, valued at £888,043. In the same year the State sawmills, Wood Preservation plants and Forest Products Institute produced products such as converted and dressed timber, box shooks, etc., valued at more than £800,000.

There are no important private plantations in the Union, with the exception of wattle plantations. Wattle plantations, which are found mostly in Natal, cover an area of 250,000 morgen, and the chief products of this industry are wattle bark and bark extract. Most of the crop is exported.

The Union is not nearly self-sufficient with regard to its timber requirements, and will remain a big importer of wood for construction purposes, etc., for many years to come.

Industry

Minerals. The industrial development of the Union started, as already stated, with the Kimberley Diamond Mines and the Lydenburg Gold Mining Co. in 1870-71, but it got its big momentum with the opening up of the Witwatersrand goldfields in 1886, ' the biggest thing the world has seen.'

Within three years, i.e., by the end of 1889 there were fifty-two working companies with an output of 300,000 oz. per year, and some 25,000 Europeans and 15,000 Natives on the Rand.

During the decade 1940-50 the output varied between 11 and 14 million ounces, and the labour force included in 1947 41,000 Europeans and about 318,700 Natives and other coloured persons.

Already in 1892 gold surpassed diamonds in value of output, and in 1932 diamonds was passed for a second time by coal;

the fourth important mineral of the Union—copper following far behind. See Table IX.

TABLE IX
Value of Mineral Output in the Union in 1947 in £ S.A. Thousands

Mineral				Output in £ S.A. Thousands
1. Gold ...	...	...	...	96,600
2. Coal ...	...	...	...	8,690
3. Diamonds	...	...	...	7,170
4. Copper ...	...	...	...	3,150
Total four main minerals	...	...	...	115,610
5. Asbestos ...	...	...	...	980
6. Manganese	...	...	...	890
7. Chrome ...	...	...	...	790
8. Platinum ...	...	...	...	650
9. Iron ore ...	...	...	...	570
10. Antimony ...	...	...	...	320
11. Silver ...	...	...	...	220
12. Tin ...	...	...	...	220
13. Other minerals	...	...	...	670
Grand Total	...			120,920

The manpower in the production of minerals is distributed as in Table X.

TABLE X
Number of Persons Employed in Mineral Production

Production of			In Thousands	In 1947	
			Europeans	Non-Europeans	Total
1. Gold			41·0	318·7	359·7
2. Coal			3·2	48·0	51·2
3. Diamonds			2·0	7·5	9·5
4. Copper			0·7	5·3	6·0
5. Other minerals			5·1	42·3	47·4
Grand Total			52·0	421·8	473·8

The percentage of national income earned in mining has gradually fallen. In the fiscal year 1911-12 it was according to the estimate of Prof. Frankel as high as 27.5 per cent and gold alone 19.6 per cent. In the fiscal year 1948-49 it was no more than 11.2 per cent and gold alone 8.5 per cent.[1]

Mining activity, apart from a few well-defined exceptions (see below) has been developed entirely by private initiative under the general supervision of the State. The somewhat sophisticated mining legislation, mainly incorporated in the Precious and Base Metals Act of 1908, the Precious Stones Act of 1927, amended in 1937, and the regulations of each of the four Provinces can easily give a wrong impression as to what actually happens. In no case, apart from the few exceptions referred to, has the State assumed direct control of mining operations. The State however, irrespective of certain partial restrictions connected with private ownership of the land, is owner of all minerals and all mining rights. The State sells these rights, outright or for an annuity or, more often, leases them to persons or companies, who have satisfied the State after a call for tenders that they possess the necessary capital and technical staff to exploit a certain area.

The leases for gold mines are based on the formula $y = a - \dfrac{b}{x}$

where :

y is the percentage of profits payable to the State;

x is the ratio of profits to the value of precious metals produced;

a and b are specific constants agreed upon in the lease.

For the calculation of profits due allowance is made for amortization of capital expenditure.

The constants a and b vary greatly with the particular circumstances. In the big majority of cases a is between 10 and 30, but values as high as 50 to 80 occur. In the last-mentioned cases b is usually higher, so that as a rule for a 10 per cent profit on

---

[1] The *South African Journal of Economics*, 1944, p. 112. It is to be kept in mind that the percentages for gold are very unsteady. When the general price level falls and the price of gold remains constant, the volume of gold production increases and gold production measured as a percentage of national income increases *a fortiori*.

output, y is between 5 and 10. In some cases a minimum percentage of profits is payable to the State.

Anyway, by these methods of exploitation the State can never be involved in any risk of loss, whilst in private industry the incentive remains to increase efficiency.[1]

In the case of the exceptionally rich diamond fields however, disclosed in 1927 in Namaqualand, i.e., the N.W. corner of the Cape Province, between the mouth of the Orange River and Port Nolloth, the alluvial deposits are worked directly by the State. In 1926 an area along the coast of 60 miles by 15 was wired in and closed to public access. It is a kind of national treasure house to be exploited in due time.

To avoid overproduction of diamonds the Government is also empowered by the Precious Stones Act and the Diamond Control Act of 1925 to control the production and sale of diamonds both from mines and from alluvial diggings. These powers however, have never been used, as the producers themselves have come to satisfactory agreements. A Diamond Board has been set up as a basis for co-operation between Government and private enterprise.

All other cases of direct State interest in mining are confined to special circumstances, e.g., State Co-operation in the mining of tungsten during the war and the Act on Atomic Energy of 1948 which reserves all rights to search, prospect, mine or extract uranium, thorium, etc., to the State.

Electric Power

All developments in this field and in the next one are connected with the name of Dr. H. J. van der Bijl, an exceptionally gifted Afrikaans engineer and scientist, who was appointed in 1921 by the then Prime Minister, General J. C. Smuts, as scientific and technical advisor to the S.A. Government.

The extent to which the prosperity of the country depended on gold and diamonds was for van der Bijl a cause for the greatest concern. He saw rightly that an iron and steel industry and a generally available and cheap supply of power are the prime conditions for developing scores of secondary industries— an approach now generally accepted by everybody in the Union.

[1] For further information the reader is referred to C. W. Biccard Jeppe. *Gold Mining in S.A.*, 1948.

In the beginning of the twenties the only large electricity supply system was owned by The Victoria Falls and Transvaal Power Co. Ltd. This Company was supplying power to the gold mines of the Rand and to most of the towns in this region. It owned four inter-connected power stations.

In 1923, based on the Electricity Act of 1922, the Electricity Supply Commission (Escom) was established. It is a mixture of State Control and private enterprise. Escom has no formal monopoly. It is financed entirely by fixed interest-bearing capital and it has to be operated on a basis of no profit or loss.

The members of the Commission are appointed by the Governor General and can be replaced by him. The initial capital of £ S.A. 8 million, was borrowed from the Union Treasury at somewhat above 5 per cent interest. After ten years of successful operation Escom started with the floatation of its own loans on the public market of the Union, so that in 1933 and 1934 the initial loan was paid back to the Government.

All extensions since have been financed in the same way; its present capital amounts to £ S.A. 50 million, all publicly subscribed.

In 1948 it took over all the assets of the Victoria Falls and Transvaal Power Co. for £ S.A. 14.5 million. Escom now owns twelve large power stations with a total installed capacity of nearly 2 million k.w.

Iron and Steel

The production of iron and steel started in 1912-13 on a small scale with the working up of railway scrap by the Union Steel Corporation at Vereeniging; in 1917 Delfos started the first experimental blast furnace in Pretoria, working on S.A. ores.

The Bounties Act of 1923 granted a premium of 15sh. per ton on all iron and steel produced from indigenous ores provided the works had a capacity of at least 50,000 tons per year. In 1938 this Act was replaced by the Iron and Steel Industry Act introduced by the Hertzog Government against strong opposition by Smuts and his followers. The Act provided for the formation of the S.A. Iron and Steel Corporation (Iscor), which started production in 1934 under the leadership of Dr. van der Bijl. The original plan to finance Iscor with 300,000 A shares of £1 each held by the Government and 9,900,000 B shares offered for public subscription did not succeed. The amount taken up by the public was very small, so that the Government had to take the big majority of the B shares as well. The B shares not held by the Government, in round figures 220,000, were converted in 1937 into 7½ per cent cumulative preference shares to permit the payment of reasonable dividends to private shareholders when Government policy should require the distribution of only low dividends on the ordinary shares. The initial issue of £ S.A. 1.5 million 5 per cent first mortgage debentures was redeemed in 1947.

The members of the Board of Directors are appointed by the Governor General.

Iscor has complete control of, or at least a substantial interest in, The Union Steel Corporation, African Metals, National Chemical Products, Van der Bijl Engineering Corporation and others.

The extension at Van der Bijl Park will have an ingot capacity of 350,000 tons, which will bring the ingot capacity of the Union's steel industry to 1,100,000 tons and the aggregate capacity of rolled steel production to 820,000 tons.

Immediately after production started in 1934 the international Steel Cartel inaugurated a systematic dumping campaign especially in the field of rail prices. Accordingly it was provided by law in 1936 that average c.i.f. world prices at Union harbours can be determined and that the difference between these prices and actual c.i.f. prices may be assessed as a duty. In 1937 however the international level of steel prices had risen considerably so that up till now duties of this kind have not been collected. An agreement between Iscor and the Cartel fell away after the outbreak of war.

The ore for the Pretoria Works is obtained from the adjacent fields and partly from a very rich and pure deposit at Thabazimbi (Mountain of Iron), acquired by Iscor. The coke ovens use 75 per cent Transvaal and 25 per cent Natal coal from private collieries. The total production of coke in the Union is close to a million tons per year. By-products such as tar, benzol, ammonium, etc., have given rise to allied privately owned industries.

Transport

As in every country the Post, Telegraphs and Telephone service is carried on by the State; this for several years has been an important source of Treasury revenue. The city of Durban still retains its own Municipal telephone business : there is however a strong movement to merge it with the State service.

The railways and harbours (S.A.R. & H.) have been owned by the State since the Anglo-Boer war, and this has been incorporated in the South Africa Act of 1909. The S.A.R. & H. virtually operate a monopoly, and their field of activity has gradually been extended to inter-urban road motor transport and the commercial air service; they have gradually taken over all regular airlines within the Union. They have also developed certain sidelines, e.g., the promotion of tourist traffic; the erection of grain elevators, etc. The railways workshops constitute the biggest engineering unit in the country. The scheme of acquiring forests for the supply of railways sleepers was abandoned in 1934 because steel of Iscor had taken the place of wood.

The tariff policy of the railways is broadly laid down in the S.A. Act of 1909. Section 127 and 128 stipulate that the railway monopoly should be administered on business principles. They are to be operated on the basis of no profit or loss but with due recognition of the agricultural and industrial development of the Union, promoting by means of cheap transport inland settlement in all provinces of the Union.

Thus the railway rates show a discrimination between nine groups of goods and a rather sharp decline per ton-mile for long hauls. Moreover so-called distribution rates exist for about forty-five scheduled inland distribution towns to diminish or to nullify the advantages otherwise enjoyed by the ports. The ' nearest port ' rates ensure certain inland manufacturers that the freight for specified goods to a certain destination within the Union will not be higher than from the nearest port to that same destination with, of course, a certain minimum ton-mile rate prescribed beyond a fixed distance.

As the Union is a sparsely populated country with long hauls and a complete lack of waterways one can safely say that the railway rates are of more importance for economic development than in most other countries. Broadly speaking they are in accordance with the Government's policy of stimulating agricultural and base metal mining. It is clear, however, that special advantages to certain groups impose an extra burden on the others, and so the railway rates are often contested by the gold mines, wholesalers and secondary industries.

Competition of private motor traffic was met by the Motor Carrier Transportation Act of 1930, amended in 1932. Each business may use its own motor vehicles for the transport of its own goods only within the magisterial district wherein the business is situated; for the conveyance of farm products and requisites there are somewhat larger exemptions. But apart from this motor carriers operating for reward must be in possession of a certificate issued by the Central Road Transportation Board or one of its local Boards. This certificate regulates the nature of the goods to be carried, dual purpose or passenger service, frequency, volume, route and period of operation. The law only affects the transport in certain specified regions or along specified routes, but these specifications include the big bulk of all inland motor transport in the Union; only the remote parts are exempted.

Opinions vary concerning the effects of the Transportation Act. At least it seems to have lessened considerably the competition with the railways.

South African Shipping till the end of the last war consisted only of some vessels owned by the railways for the supply of wooden sleepers from Australia. In 1946 it got a new impetus by the establishment of the S.A. Marine Corporation on an entirely private basis. Its formation was largely due to the initiative of Dr. van der Bijl. Its issued capital is £ S.A. 0.8 million; about 60 per cent of this amount is held locally while a large interest has been acquired by the States Marine Corporation of New York, one of the biggest shipping lines in U.S.A. As a start, three Victory Ships of about 15,000 tons each were bought and transformed into combined cargo and passenger ships. The main outward cargo is South African ore.

In the same year the Alpha S.A. Steam Ship Co. was established with an issued capital of £ S.A. 0.6 million. It is controlled by the Moller Group, Hong Kong, and owns four ships with a total tonnage of about 45,000 tons.

Apart from these two there are nine other companies. The S.A. fleet at the middle of 1949 consisted of 31 ships with a total tonnage of 135,000 tons. This figure does not include the smaller coasters, which however play a very important role for the inter-connection of S.A. ports.

There is no State interference or subsidizing of shipping.

Secondary Industries

As in every new country the industrial development in its early stages was confined to typical local production and industries directly connected with the cultivation of the soil, such as milking, baking, wine and brandy industry, fruit-preserving and beer-brewing.

TABLE XI

Number of Persons Employed in Secondary Industry In Thousands

Year	Europeans	Non-Europeans	Total
1911	21·0	44·9	65·9
1920	62·9	116·9	179·8
1930	90·9	127·4	218·3
1940	143·5	216·9	360·4
1946	178·5	341·1	519·6
1950	236·5	369·0	605·5

In Natal, however, as early as 1852 the first steam-driven sugar mill was erected; the output of 3,500 tons of sugar in 1860 increased to 20,000 in 1890 and more than 500,000 tons in 1948. Expansion to 725,000 is in preparation. On balance the Union has now become a sugar exporting country. An import duty of £16 per ton was in 1948 temporarily suspended.

The expansion of S.A. industry excluding mining and quarrying, roughly measured by the number of persons employed, is given in Table XI. The Table clearly shows that during the period 1920-30 the development slowed down and during this period, accordingly, a series of measures have been taken by the Government to speed it up. We mentioned above the nomination of Dr. van der Bijl in 1921 as Advisor to the Government.

In 1924 the Board of Trade and Industries was established as a successor to the Industrial Board of 1916. It consists of five full-time members appointed by the Minister of Commerce and Industry for a period of five years with possibility of renewal. Its task is to advise the Government concerning all questions related to the economic development of the Union and especially, inter alia, concerning premiums and subsidies to industries, tariff policy, the effects of trusts and combines, monopolies and mischievous restraints of trade, dumping policies, etc.

In 1925 the Revised Customs Tariff Act embodied the Government's policy of promoting industrial development in every field. The tariff is subject to annual revision, so that for new industries tariffs could be lowered after a certain initial period; lack of efficiency and undue high prices can be counteracted in the same way.

Benefits derived from these measures, however useful, were surpassed by those flowing from two circumstances which have given the industrial development of the Union a major impetus during the last two decades, viz., the exceptional expansion of gold mining after the devaluation of the S.A. Pound at the end of 1932 and the rise of the American gold price in March, 1933, and the second World War.

Manufacturing, which accounted, according to the figures of Prof. Frankel, in 1911-12 for only 6.8 per cent of the national income, which figure had risen to 10.5 in 1919-20 and to 15.2 in 1929-30, represented 17.6 per cent in 1939-40 and 23.4 per cent in 1948-49. The rate of development of manufacturing accordingly was bigger than that in all other fields. The index of production as calculated by the Standard Bank of S.A. on the 1934-1938 average = 1,000 rose for the year 1949 to 1,856 but for manufacturing to 2,557, i.e., the highest value out of the seven groups from which this index is compounded.

This very favourable development took place mainly in the sectors of building materials (cement, bricks, tiles, corrugated steel plate, etc.), textiles and clothing, shoe production (the import of shoes after the war had almost disappeared) and in the engineering trades.

From the 520,000 employed in manufacturing in 1946 nearly one-third are working in metal engineering, machinery, etc., so that the country is now to a very large extent producing its own investment goods. The output of this industry includes nearly all lines such as batteries, springs, glowlamps, etc. Only tools and machinery of a highly specialized character need still to be imported.

The prices often compare favourably with those of the older industrial countries; the rise in retail prices and cost of living in the Union has been one of the smallest in the world. The prices of Iscor, e.g., which were before the war some 5 per cent below U.S.A. and Great Britain inland prices, are now 40-50 per cent lower. Coal and electric power are in South Africa cheaper than anywhere else.

It should be emphasized that the establishment of new enterprises of any kind is not subject to restrictions except in the baking and milling trade, liquor stores, etc.

Large numbers of the new industries have been established with the aid of British firms by means of capital participation, specialized machinery, technical assistance, leading staff and skilled workmen. There is however, a growing tendency for other countries to contribute to the development; the U.S.A. in the first place, but also Belgium, France, Germany, Holland, Italy, Switzerland and others. And apart from that several industries are built upon a purely South African basis, often by English-speaking people, but to a nincreasing degree by Afrikaans-speaking people as well.

From the early beginnings there has been a marked difference between the role of these two groups in business, the Afrikaners being mainly engaged in agriculture, public service, railways, etc., the English in mining, industry, commerce, banking and insurance. This difference is gradually and slowly decreasing and one of the most prominent changes is taking place in secondary industries, where the Afrikaans-speaking section is rapidly expanding. Particular influence in this direction has been exercised by the *Ekonomiese Volkskongres* of 1939. The establishment of the *Handelsinstituut* after that date has contributed largely to push up the Afrikaans-speaking section of the population to a more important and active role in the economic field.

Shortly after the outbreak of war in 1939 a commission was appointed to survey the Union's industrial and agricultural requirements and to inquire into the development of S.A. resources, under the chairmanship of Dr. van Eck. Its report has led to the establishment in 1941 of the Economic Advisory and Planning Council acting in an advisory capacity to the Cabinet, through the Prime Minister, in regard to the social and economic programmes of the State. This Planning Council therefore has no executive power. Its main task is to study the policy of the numerous specialized boards, departments and semi-public bodies with a view to co-ordinate and fuse their major activities into a unified policy.

Already in October 1940 the Industrial Development Cor-- poration of S.A. had been established under the chairmanship of Dr. van Eck, to facilitate and to assist others in the financing of new industries and the expansion or modernization of existing industries. From the authorized capital of £ S.A. 5 millions, nearly three millions have been issued, all subscribed by the Government. The Corporation's activities are confined to assist- ing secondary industries, thus precluding any activity in the field of farming, mining and pure trading. It has taken a particular interest in textile manufacturing (wool and cotton), the produc- tion of animal feeds and food yeast. It has underwritten several industrial share issues to the public, and some of the under- takings previously operated by the Corporation have since been transferred to private ownership.

In 1945, immediately after the peace, two important new institutions were established by Act of Parliament, the Council for Scientific and Industrial Research and the Standards Council.

The former finds its task in the development and co-ordination of all research work in the Union and has to keep it constantly on an international level. It has established laboratories for physical and chemical research, the national bureau for personal research, an institute for building research and a laboratory for research in the field of tele-communications. It is in permanent contact with the research departments of the Universities and of certain trade associations.

The Standards Council and its executive branch the S.A. Bureau of Standards, unlike similar institutions abroad, is entirely financed by the Government; the Government, accordingly, appoints the seven members of the Council. It is a salient point in its policy to maintain the fullest possible liaison with all organizations working on standardization all over the world.

It has particularly close relations with the S.A. Standards Institution, which is entirely based on private initiative and covers almost the same field as the Standards Council. To ensure perfect co-ordination a Joint Committee has been established which considers all applications for standardization and allocates the work either to the S.A. Standards Institution or to the Standards Council. The underlying reason for this somewhat complicated procedure is to establish a certain harmony and equilibrium between British and non-British influences.

An important point in this field is the difference between the British system of weights and measures and the decimal metric system. A report concerning this problem was published in 1948. As a first step the decimalization of the monetary system is now under consideration.

Banking and Finance

The dominant position of the British sector and the gradual development of the other sector is most clearly reflected in the private banking system. Practically the whole banking business is done by four concerns. Of these the two British banks— Barclays Bank and Standard Bank—are by far the most important; each of them has about 350-400 branch offices, agencies, etc. The Nederlandsche Bank voor Z.A. (Dutch) has 24 and Volkskas, which had 28 branches when it was recognized as a commercial bank in 1940, now have about 77 branches.

The S.A. Reserve Bank is as a Central bank operated under Government control. The drastic concentration of private banking makes it relatively easy to attain a co-ordinated policy. Thus the measures of import control introduced in 1948-49 to re-establish the equilibrium in the balance of payments after the over-expansion during the post-war period were put into effect without too much trouble. The situation improved still further after the revaluation of the S.A. £ in September, 1949.

Broadly speaking one may state that the financial equilibrium of the Union is pretty stable. Nearly all Government loans abroad, which were so important in the early years of the Union, and which reached a maximum about 1933, have by now been repaid; all short term loans are financed within the Union, and the foreign debt of municipalities is not excessive. The amount of interest and dividends paid to outside owners is now estimated at about £36 million.

The establishment by the Government of the National Finance Corporation with a capital of £ S.A. 1 million, has provided a useful supplement to the Union's financial system. It absorbs liquid assets at a low interest rate and invests in Union Treasury Bills and other Government Securities with a maturity not exceeding five years.

Characteristic of the Union is the somewhat speculative spirit of its white population. The symptoms are found in the very long list of the Johannesburg Stock Exchange, the buying of shares more for capital appreciation than for net return, the speculation in building plots and the more or less chronic over-buying by the average citizen. This last tendency is favoured by systems of hire-purchase applied not only to motor cars, furniture, etc., but also to all kinds of clothing.

Consumers' Co-operative Societies had only 100,000 members in 1947-48, and a total business turnover of £5.5 million.

Although adequate figures are lacking, it seems as if savings as a percentage of national income are not lower in the Union than in comparable countries, and that the dependency of the country on foreign capital imports is gradually decreasing.

The one-sidedness of the Union's economy, due to the early development of gold mining, is diminishing. In 1938 the percentage of issued capital for gold mines was 43.5 per cent of all issued capital quoted on the Johannesburg Stock Exchange; in 1949 it was only 26.0 per cent. (See Table XII.) The Market value of gold shares in 1938 was 61 per cent and in 1949 43.3 per cent of the total.

Public Finance

The Union's financial position, as shown above, is fundamentally sound. The net public debt of the Union Government as at 31st March, 1949, was £662 million. Of this amount £459.5 million has been spent on interest-earning assets, £86 million on permanent, non-interest earning assets, and the balance on war and other unproductive projects.

The Union Government usually has surpluses on current account. Its revenue in 1948-49 was obtained from the following sources: £46.4 million (customs and excise); £87.3 million (Inland Revenue, mostly direct taxation) and £13.1 million from its Post and Telegraphs department.

TABLE XII
Johannesburg Stock Exchange 1938–1949

	Number of Companies Quoted		Issued Capital in Million Pounds		Market Value of Shares quoted in Million Pounds	
	31.12.38	31.12.49	31.12.38	31.12.49	31.12.38	31.12.49
Gold producers	44	52	52·7	68·5	276·3	355·8
Non-producers	42	49	32·8	52·3	57·3	255·3
Total... ...	86	101	85.5	120·8	333·6	611·1
Diamonds	14	8	12·1	13·2	22·8	62·8
Collieries	11	20	5·2	11·3	9·4	35·0
Base metals	14	11	11·6	13·0	12·2	39·3
Total... ...	125	140	114·4	158·3	378·0	748·2
Financial	22	67	43·6	100·0	105·1	315·1
Industrial	61	355	29·0	185·5	44·0	312·1
Supplementary	18	43	3·3	11·8	2·4	12·4
Banks	3	3	8·0	10·6	18·4	28·0
Total... ...	229	608	198·3	466·2	547·9	1,415·8
Government and Municipal Stock	35	101	118·7	573·8	121·0	546·5
Debentures	1	—	4·9	2·2	5·0	2·1
Convertible notes ...	—	—	1·0	1·2	1·4	1·2
Preferred stock	—	—	2·4	3·7	2·8	4·6
Grand Total ...	265	709	325·3	1,047·1	678·1	1,970·2

The soundness of these investments is shown by the index Market value divided by Issued capital, which amounted to 2.76 in 1938 and 3.02 in 1949.

The industrial share index (1938 = 100) was 178.5 in April 1950, which compares favourably with the similar figure for London at the same date of 122 and for New York of 167.

The Union Government is engaged upon a vast investment programme at present. Its expenditure on loan account in 1948-49 totalled £77.7 million (including advances to the S.A. Railways for capital expenditure). The capital expenditure of local Government has been to the order of approximately £19 million in the 1948 financial year. The Provincial Governments obtain their funds for current and capital expenditure from taxation and grants from the Union Government.

Labour Conditions in the Union

A corollary of the racial hierarchy that exists in the Union's labour market is the 'skill structure' of the labour force. From the beginning of the Union's modern development skilled work has been associated with the European, on account of his better training and his higher standard of living. Unskilled work was reserved for the non-Europeans. Coloureds in the Cape Province and Indians in Natal have made some headway in skilled occupations, but in the case of the Native, whose tribal background does not prepare him for the way of life of Western industrial society, little advance has been made; and where the necessary skill has been acquired the structure of the Trade Unions does not permit his entry into the 'skilled workers' category.

The skill structure in the industries subject to wage determinations of the Wage Board over the period 1937-1947 is apparent from Table XIII. The total number of workers of all races involved was 233,200, and of this number about one-third was skilled, and just under one-half unskilled.

Only 2.1 per cent of the European workers belonged to the unskilled class, and 81.4 per cent were skilled. Just the reverse is observed in the case of the Natives. Here 4.1 per cent were skilled and 83.2 per cent unskilled. Asiatics showed a much higher percentage of skilled workers than the other non-European races.

There is a definite tendency, however, for the non-Europeans to increase their numbers in semi-skilled class of jobs. In the Wage Board sample 34.2 per cent of the Europeans belonged to this class, so that two-thirds of the semi-skilled workers were non-Europeans. The European workers formed 84.1 per cent of all the skilled workers and 2.1 per cent of all the unskilled workers in the Wage Board sample.

TABLE XIII

Percentage Distribution, According to Skill, of Workers in Industries Subject to Wage Determinations, Wage Board, 1937-1947

Type of Worker	Europeans	Natives	Asiatics	Coloureds	All Races
	%	%	%	%	%
Skilled	81·4	4·1	31·9	14·5	34·0
Semi-skilled	16·5	12·7	32·2	30·7	18·0
Unskilled...	2·1	83·2	35·9	54·8	48·0
Totals	100	100	100	100	100

Source : U.G. 38/1949, p. 45.

The disparity between skilled and unskilled wages in the Union, viz., a proportion of 5 : 1, is bigger than that of Western countries. This gap cannot be narrowed unless opportunities of better paid employment are made available to the non-Europeans, especially Natives. This widening of economic opportunity could be achieved, among other things, by a programme of industrialization in the Native Reserves. As skilled work in the European sector has always been considered the preserve of the Europeans, trade union pressure would make it difficult for non-Europeans to enter the skilled trades in any big numbers. *There are no formal legal barriers against the entry of the skilled trades by Natives, except in the case of certain operations in the mining industry.* One reason why the unskilled wage has been so low in relation to the skilled wage is that in the past the supply of Native labour in the European labour market has been well-nigh perfectly elastic at the current wage rate. The continuous influx of Natives from the impoverished reserves served to keep this basic wage for unskilled work pegged at its low level. At the same time the labour market experienced a recurring shortage of skilled labour. This deficient supply has not been met to a sufficient extent by immigration from abroad. The streamlining of apprenticeship regulations, so far not adapted to the needs of a growing industrial society, may help to ease the situation.

The collective bargaining process in the Union was provided with a legal framework by the Industrial Conciliation Act, originally passed by the Nationalist-Labour Pact Government in 1924. Agriculture, domestic service and Government employment were excepted from the provisions of this Act. Employers' and workers' unions are registered in terms of this Conciliation Act, and their agreements are legalized by proclamation. Native trade unions cannot be registered in terms of this Act, which means that they cannot participate in the collective bargaining process in the ordinary way.

By the Wage Act passed in 1925, a Wage Board was set up which recommends to the Minister of Labour what *minimum* wage and employment standards should be laid down in the industries which it investigates. The Board uses the cost of living and ability to pay as criteria for its wage determinations. As the Board theoretically may not discriminate on the basis of race or colour in making its determinations, it goes without saying that the Natives as a class stand to gain by its decisions.

The Union's industries are heavily unionized. The biggest and most influential trade union is the Mine Workers' Union. The number of members of unions registered under the Conciliation Act in 1946 was 348,434. The membership of non-registered unions, i.e., mostly members of native trade unions, was 61,648. Trade union practices, such as the closed shop rule, are regular features of the country's industrial relations, and in this field the lead is usually given by the powerful Mine Workers' Union, mentioned above.

Two other Acts dealing with the welfare of workers are the Unemployment Insurance Act of 1946 and the Workmen's Compensation Act of 1941, which make provision for the protection of workers against unemployment and industrial disability respectively.

Concluding Remarks

Without fear of contradiction it may be stated categorically that the generally accepted principle in the Union is to leave the positive economic process to private enterprise. Any departure from that central principle is regarded as a deviation which must in every instance be amply justified.

The Undue Restraint of Trade Act of 1949 is an expression of this feeling that freedom of trade should be protected as much as possible.

On the other hand the vested interests are protected not so much by legal measures as by written and unwritten conventions which often make the life of the newcomer difficult.

The lower income groups of the white population have prospered considerably since the twenties and the problem of the " poor whites " has virtually disappeared.

In the case of the Native population the chief difficulty is that they are faced with the transition from primitive tribal society to one run on Western lines. The rate of increase has been strongly influenced by better hygienic measures, but at the same time the masses, especially in the Reserves, are still given over to inherited superstitions and ruinous practices in regard to soil cultivation and cattle breeding, which undermine the very basis of their existence, and hamper economic progress in the Reserves. In addition, there is the growing problem of over-crowding.

The rate of increase of all the races in the Union has been rapid in the past. The annual rate of increase of Europeans between 1936-46 was 1.644 per cent, for Natives 1.697 per cent, for Asiatics 2.558 per cent and Coloureds 1.894 per cent. The net reproduction rate of the European during the period 1945-47 was 1.50, and for Coloured and Asiatics 1.90 and 2.35 respectively. Similar calculations cannot be made for the Natives, on account of the lack of vital statistics. All these figures indicate a very high potential population growth, especially in the case of the non-Europeans, whose death rate will be diminished further by better medical services.

To meet the needs of its growing population the Union will have to push ahead with the diversification of its economy, with the emphasis on the highest productivity per man-hour attainable within the framework of its dual society.

PROFESSOR DOCTOR JAN GOUDRIAAN

Born 1893 at Amsterdam, Holland. Mechanical engineer, 1915. Inspector of factories, 1916. Manager of the Central Bureau of

Standards, 1922. Chief Engineer, Fyenoord Shipyard, Rotterdam, 1924. Chief of Efficiency Department of Phillips concern, Eindhoven, 1928, and member of the Board of Directors, since 1933. General Manager, Dutch Railways, 1938.

During the German occupation of Holland, spent nearly two years as hostage in concentration camps.

In October 1944 was reinstated as General Manager of the Railways (had been dismissed by the Germans during the occupation). Resigned, 1945. Visited Caribbean area on official mission 1946-7.

Since 1926, part-time Professor in Business Economics at Rotterdam University and also, since 1936, at the Technical University of Delft. Since 1949, head of the Department of Business Economics at Pretoria University.

Chief Publications : Efficiency of the Bread Supply of Amsterdam (thesis), 1922; How to Stop Deflation, London, 1932; Unemployment Problem and How to Solve It (Dutch Association for Political Economy and Statistics), 1947; and numerous articles in the economic press.

PROFESSOR D. G. FRANZSEN

Born Cape Town, 1918. Finished High School training at Wellington, Cape Province, and then proceeded to the Afrikaans-medium University of Stellenbosch. Took the following degrees : B.A. (1938), M.A. (1939) and D.Phil (1942). Post-graduate study took place at the Graduate School of Public Administration, Harvard University, and at Chicago and Washington, D.C.

Lectured at Stellenbosch in the Department of Economics from 1940, and held the Economics Chair at that University from January 1947. In January 1950 took up present position, viz., Head of the Department of Economic Theory and Economic History, University of Pretoria. Has also been attached to the Statistical Department of the South African Reserve Bank for the last four years.

Principal publications : two textbooks on economics and population problems written in collaboration with Prof. Schumann and Dr. Sadie respectively; also articles on theoretical subjects in economics and memoranda on national income.

CHAPTER XII

Quo Vadis?

DAVID MARQUARD

THE concluding paragraph of the introductory chapter to this book reads as follows : ('For the past 150 years the history of South Africa has been a history of conflict. Conflict between black man and black man, between white man and black man, between white man and white man; struggle of white and black against a not over-generous nature—this is the background to its present problems.') The discerning reader of the chapters which followed that introduction will have noticed that the conflicts and struggles have in no way been resolved. In some cases the emphasis has been shifted, in others there has been a regrouping of the contestants. But it is crystal clear that there is not yet that inner harmony which is to be found in those mother countries from which the European inhabitants of South Africa are in the main descended.

It would perhaps be expecting too much to find this national harmony of ideas and ideologies in a country whose political history is of such comparatively recent date, a country which has had to reconcile within its boundaries the monarchist traditions of England, the republican traditions of the Transvaal and of the Orange Free State and the tribal traditions of a race which is in many ways only just emerging from barbarism. The statesmen of most countries are apt to consider the problems of their country as unique when these problems are in reality merely different facets of the world-wide problems of human relationships, of economic adjustment, of the growing pains of nationhood. The preceding chapters have pointed out, and pointed out aptly, in what respects the problems of South Africa may be considered as being peculiar to our country.

In Chapter II Dr. du Toit has shown that the first Dutch

colonists set themselves to maintain in their new homeland a community which would remain essentially European in blood and in culture and how they have, in the main, succeeded in this task. The result is that they formed one of the few " colonial " communities where a small European settlement has faced a large aboriginal population and has retained its identity without decimating its hosts. A comparison with the history of the colonial development of the two Americas is not an odious one, for there is no attempt to praise the one policy or damn the other; the comparison is made merely to stress the difference of the racial problems which at present face these countries. In addition, the descendants of these Dutchmen have developed a new language which differs much more from the Dutch of Holland than American does from modern English.

The English immigrants of the nineteenth and twentieth centuries, as Mr. Currey points out in the third chapter, brought to our country the industrial, commercial and political arts and crafts for which their homeland was famous. But in spite of similarities of outlook with regard to racial policy and religion, as well as a fundamental common belief in the principles of democracy, the two main European groups developed violent mutual antagonisms which have only now passed their climax. In fact, up till quite recently, the phrase ' race relations ' in South Africa was generally assumed to be the relations between the English and Afrikaans-speaking groups, and not the far more fundamental and vital relationship between the white and the coloured races.

That this latter relationship is anything but an harmonious one emerges from Chapters V to VII.

Mr. Ngcobo, in Chapter V, explains how the attitude of the Bantu towards the various sections of the Europeans differs, but does not attempt to disguise the fact that even at its best this attitude is one of suspicion, while at its worst it is one of active hostility. Messrs. Golding and Joshua develop this attitude of resentment in their description of the racial bars which exist to limit the employment of Coloured people in skilled and semi-skilled trades, and Mr. Calpin has the same story to tell about the Indian community. And yet, in the economic survey, the figures point to an ever-increasing contribution being made by non-Europeans of all races to the industrial life of the country. Finally, Mr. Prestwich points to the constitutional position and ' the attempts which have been made to reconcile the aspirations of some of the natives for a voice in matters of concern to them with the almost universal conviction of European South Africans that the Native is not ripe for self-government and that European predominance must be maintained.'

Self-government, a system of government in which the people, or at any rate a large section of the people, determines what form its political institutions should take, is a comparatively modern product. It is, further, a product of Western Europe, and it was transplanted to America, Africa and India by the great colonizing powers after the discovery of the new world. It is no historical accident that this geographical development came shortly after the Renaissance, which saw the beginning of a movement which led ultimately to universal education, and it is equally obvious that the ideal of self-government has been fertilized by the dead bones of illiteracy. Ramsay Muir postulates two main conditions for the growth of self-government : ' firstly, the mass of active citizens who take a share in the direction of affairs must be in some degree educated, not merely in the formal sense, though that is important, but still more in the sense of having been trained in the practice of co-operation in common affairs. The second condition is that there must exist a real unity of sentiment in the community which attempts self-government.'

To what degree does the South African community fulfil these two conditions? Dr. Wollheim provides part of the answer to the first condition in Chapter VIII, where his figures indicate that in 1944 562,000 African children attended schools as compared with 420,000 Europeans, the percentages of the total population being respectively 7.5 and 18.7. But it is interesting to note that only eight years previously the figures were 360,000 for Bantu (percentage 5.5) and 375,000 (18.7 per cent) and there is no reason for thinking that the process suggested by these comparative figures will ever be reversed. The number of Bantu attending universities and colleges is also steadily increasing, so that while the necessary standard of ' formal ' education for Africans has in no sense of the word yet been attained, there is every indication that illiteracy among them will, within measurable time, be a thing of the past, as it is to-day already for the European population.

What of the other type of education, that which Muir calls 'a training in the practice of co-operation in common affairs?' The tribal organization of the African, fully described in Chapter V, can hardly be said to provide this, and in any case some forty per cent of the Bantu are by now detribalized, while even in the Bantu territories themselves tribal sanctions are rapidly disappearing and the inhabitants are, on the whole, ruled over and administered by Europeans, although in the Transkei the 'Bunga,' a mixed 'parliament' consisting partly of elected Bantu and partly of nominated Bantu and Europeans, does administer the agricultural, educational and irrigation policy on behalf of some 1,250,000 Bantu. In spite of the fact that its annual funds amount to not more than £200,000, the system has been described as 'an experiment in political science, in training the Bantu to the task of local self-government.' Otherwise, as Mr. Prestwich points out, it is only in the Cape Colony that the Bantu or Coloured people have even a limited share in the government, the experiment of the Native Representative Council having failed, partly because it was given no executive powers of any sort and therefore no real responsibility.

As to the second condition for self-government—'a real unity of sentiment '—it must be abundantly clear that this condition does not exist in South Africa at present. In spite of the many differences which exist between the English and Afrikaans-speaking groups and to which attention has already been drawn —differences of political tradition, of language, of social environment—in spite of these differences, there is here a basis for a common culture, a common government. The movement of the Afrikaner to the cities, mentioned by Dr. du Toit, has tended to give the two sections of the Europeans a common outlook on economic matters; inter-marriage and education are wiping out lingual differences; an intense common love of sport is playing its part; the creation of a National Theatre, in which bilingual companies tour the country performing plays alternately in English and in Afrikaans, has done much to co-ordinate cultural activities of two groups which were at one time mutually exclusive. But the most potent unifying factor of all has been, may one say unhappily (for an alliance based on a common fear may be an uneasy one), a realization, which has only become evident in the past few years, that the satisfactory solution of the problem of the relationship between white and black is a far, far more important matter than Anglo-Afrikaans rivalry. For almost a century contact between the Bantu and the Afrikaner was a matter of frontier politics, while contact between the English-speaking South African and the Bantu was not. Now that the Bantu and the Afrikaner have both been urbanized, the two sections of the European population are both faced with the same problem, as is, of course, the most important element in the whole problem, the Bantu himself : how can relations between the two groups be stabilized so as to give satisfaction to both? Race relations have at last come to mean relations between Black and White. But since power, political and economic, is in the hands of the European section of the population, it is that section which will have to decide on the method of stabilization. In the concluding paragraph of his chapter, Dr. Wollheim states the problem from the educational point of view; his words might well be applied to the problem in general. ‘When 11,000,000 people of four different cultural origins, speaking a dozen different languages, and on every rung of the ladder of literacy and civilization, must live together in amity, solutions are not easily found.’ Before looking at two of the solutions which find the widest support in South Africa, it is perhaps necessary to stress the fact that the country is in the throes of its Industrial Revolution, one of the chief aspects of which is, of course, a large scale urbanization, in this case of the Bantu. This process always has far-reaching results, but in South Africa its implications, social and economic, are phenomenal. Its extent is indicated by the fact that the urban Bantu population has virtually doubled in the past ten years, that the number of Bantu employed in secondary industries has actually increased by 110 per cent since just before the war. What is more important, perhaps, is the fact that over a million Bantu have been pitchforked straight from a tribal life into a highly industrialized community. In the Bantu Reserves from which they come, they have been accustomed to a life where tribal sanctions rule, where the economy has been a subsistence economy, where there has been virtually no awareness of the complications of life in a modern industrial community. They have had their own tribal codes, of course, but these are based on tribal law and custom, a very different thing from European law and custom. Further, a large number of the urban Bantu are men who have had to leave their wife (or wives) and families behind them in the Reserves, there to till the fields and look after the cattle : labour is, in fact, the chief item of export of these territories.

In the industrial area the wifeless husband lives in a special compound—a labour camp on a permanent basis—or in one of the Bantu townships. He has to adapt himself quickly to his new job, which is in itself a big task, for it is a job which probably involves working with some type of machine—from a vacuum cleaner upwards. He is hurled, in fact, from a primitive era straight into the machine age and is expected to learn in a couple of years what the European urban population has taken generations to acquire.

But he also has to adapt himself to the morals, to the code of behaviour, to the laws of his new environment. Very often he has to do so alone, for there is seldom provision in the township —and never in the mine compounds—for his family, and the family unit plays a most important part in the life of the tribal Bantu. His housing conditions are usually woefully inadequate, as they are in all new industrial cities, and the result is that the standard of sexual morality, high among the tribal Bantu, is deplorably low in the cities. It is not surprising, too, that crime and disease follow close in the wake of the break-up of family life and of poor housing, and it is interesting to note that the native township of Port Elizabeth, which provides ample sub-sidized housing schemes and enables the family unit to be retained, has been remarkably free of petty crime.

The city worker quickly acquires the superficialities of white civilization, and illiteracy disappears more readily in the urban areas than in the reserves. As he learns to read his own and European papers, as he gets opportunities to listen to the radio and to attend cinemas, the urban Bantu must inevitably begin to ask himself what the future holds for him. His wage, as an unskilled worker, is roughly from one-fifth to one-third of that of the European, and he is hindered by statute from becoming a ' skilled ' worker in the technical sense of the word. His recreational facilities, while they are expanding, are negligible compared to those of the Europeans; his educational opportunities are limited; he has no share in the government of his own town; he is ' outside the pale of the constitution.' His movement from place to place is controlled by urban authorities, and all Natives, with few exceptions, are forced to carry ' passes ' or identity cards which must be produced on the demand of any member of the Police.

Most of the laws and regulations governing the Bantu have their origin in the days when he was a great deal nearer to barbarism than he is to-day, and the modern Bantu has come to resent them and resent them fiercely, as Mr. Ngcobo suggests. This resentment has as yet hardly ever broken out into open protest, but it is there nevertheless. It is a growing awareness of this feeling of resentment that has brought home to the European community the urgency of the problem of race relations in the country generally but especially in the urban areas.

On the other hand, the cash wages of the Bantu as a whole have increased considerably during the past quarter of a century, and this has made him a very much more important person, for he has become a purchaser of manufactured goods, and the commercial community, which now includes a large proportion of the Afrikaans-speaking section of the people, appreciates this fact.

Not only commercial men but the whole population appreciates too the fact that the Bantu provide them with comparatively cheap labour for domestic and industrial work. In other words, the European community as a whole would find it extremely difficult to do without the Bantu, whether as labourer or as purchaser. Equally, of course, the Bantu would find it extremely difficult to get on without the European as organizer, as teacher, as foreman. If, then, the two main groups—leaving the Coloured and Indian communities aside for the moment—are mutually inter-dependent, and if they both realize the extent of this need, where does the problem come in? Its origins lie deep in the history of the country, when the white man, Christian and bearing the banner of Western civilization, was threatened with extinction by the Bantu, heathen and barbaric; when the Bantu, simple and living a pastoral community life, saw in the white man an enemy who threatened his very existence. There was born that mutual fear and distrust which generations of both races have inherited. The fact that since then white men have given to their black compatriots education, medical care, religious instruction, and many of the opportunities which the amenities of Western civilization have to offer; that black men have helped their white compatriots to mine the gold, to build the railways, to till the fields, essential work without which the development of South Africa would have been impossible—none of these has as yet been able to exorcise the devil of fear. To scoff at fear and to ridicule it is perhaps the right way to treat it, but not always the easy way; it is certainly no good to pretend that it is not there.

There are two main approaches to the solution of this, South Africa's greatest problem: they can be roughly but fairly accurately summed up in the words integration and differentiation. Neither word is fully explanatory; each word needs some qualification.

The government which is at present in power is attempting to apply the principle of differentiation (to which it gives the Afrikaans name of Apartheid, meaning literally separateness) and it is therefore as well to start with that.

According to its apostles, Apartheid means that there must be certain areas of South Africa which must be reserved for Europeans and certain other areas which must be reserved for the Bantu. In the former areas, only white men would be entitled to own land, to maintain industries, to run the civil service, to operate businesses; the black man would be admitted as a visitor and a worker only. He would be compelled to live in certain defined areas, to work in certain defined trades only; and above all he would not be entitled to the rights of citizenship with all that that term involves. Correspondingly, the Bantu areas would be reserved for the Bantu; white men would not be allowed to own land, to operate businesses, to direct companies or to be civil servants, unless they were specifically invited to do so. Equally, they would not be allowed to obtain citizen rights in this area, but would be treated, like the Bantu in the white territory, as a visitor. But there is this qualification: the Bantu, at his present stage of development, social, commercial, political and educational, would not be able to undertake the complete running of his own territory, and the white man would therefore have to do this for him, gradually, however, training him to perform the hundred and one duties which the running of a modern community involves. There would therefore be a gradual withdrawal of European control until such time as the Bantu would be the masters in their own autonomous state.

As this is a long-term policy, its protagonists prefer to leave open the difficult and critical question, to be answered when the time comes, as to what the relationship between the two states, the European and the Bantu state, will be. On the whole, too, they leave unanswered, at the moment, the very important question of where the boundaries between the states will be drawn, and one of the main criticisms of the scheme is that the present Bantu Reserves are wholly inadequate and that the Europeans would have to be prepared to surrender much of the territory which they now hold, a surrender which will not be lightly made. On the other hand some of the more extreme differentiationists maintain that this sacrifice ought to be made and that even black labour ought to be excluded from the new 'white' state. But that is definitely a minority view: the majority realizes that industry in South Africa can only be run with the help of the African and maintains that his labour should therefore be retained, but that he should have no citizenship rights at all.

Opposed to this policy is the Integrationist school of thought which sees no future in the Balkanization of the country, and which in any case considers it to be impracticable. It sees the population of the country, not as so many Europeans and so many non-Europeans, but as eleven million human beings. The industries, the farms, the mines of the country, says the integrationist, need the labour and the managerial ability of all these people, and the sooner the whole population has reached the stage where it can play its full part in the task of developing the country, the better. As long as three-quarters of the population is under-educated and under-paid, so, long will they be a liability and not an asset to the country. It would be possible, further, to let this integration go hand in hand with social differentiation; that is, there could still be different residential areas for black and white, there could still be different schools and colleges, there need be no race mixture—for this is one thing which neither black nor white in the country desire. And what of civil rights? Will the Bantu be given full citizenship status in South Africa? This question all but a small minority of integrationists hesitate to answer, for they know that if they say ' yes,' which should be their logical answer, the ultimate result must be that they will become a minority in what they consider to be their homeland, while they also know that they cannot give to the Bantu all the privileges of Western civilization and then deny him the ultimate privilege of exercising his franchise. And they are afraid that if he does acquire the franchise, white domination in South Africa will be finished. It is not the first time in history that a ruling group has been called upon to make this fateful decision : it has had to be made in England, in France—in fact, in almost every country of the world. In South Africa, the question is more complicated by virtue of the fact that racial feelings play a determining part—and while one may deplore racialism, it is no good pretending that it does not exist.

This is the position as viewed from the European point of view : how does it look from the other side of the fence? The Bantu can, it should be clear, give only one answer. To him, South Africa is his only fatherland. Tribalism is a dying force and is being replaced by Bantu nationalism, the growth of which is at present slow, but the rate of growth is accelerating. ' Bantu nationalism,' says Mr. Ngcobo in Chapter V, ' refuses to accept the ideas of inferiority and believes in the capacity of the Bantu.' There is therefore no doubt as to what the answer of the Bantu will be when they are posed the question : Differentiation or Integration?

The full exploitation of the mineral resources of the country; the conquest of soil erosion, which is converting great portions of South Africa into a dust bowl; the creation of a great body of secondary industries which will supply southern Africa as far as the Equator and further; all these are urgent problems which must be tackled if the Union of South Africa is to fulfil its

destiny of leading the southern half of the Dark Continent into
the light of modern civilization. But their solution, their full and
adequate solution, depends on the answer to the great question
of race relations : how is the energy, the initiative and the organizing ability of the white race to be harnessed to the natural gifts
of the Bantu so that the two groups will be able to work together
for the development of their country? On the answer to this
question depends the future of the South African nation.

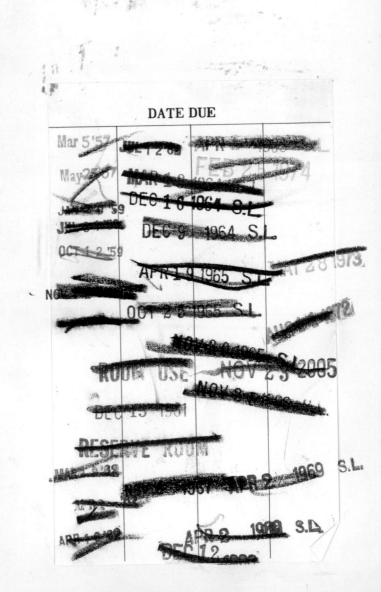

DATE DUE